EVALUATING
TRAINING

Peter Bramley

Peter Bramley is a lecturer in the Department of Organisational Psychology at Birkbeck College, the University of London. From 1964 to 1981, when he joined Birkbeck, he was an officer in the British Army, specialising in training-related issues. While serving he took a BSc in psychology at Exeter University and studied for an MPhil and PhD (the main theme of which was recognition training) at Birkbeck. His work there has included setting up the Centre for Training and Evaluation Studies, a research and consultancy group that has helped to evaluate training procedures for British Gas, the Army, the Civil Service, Shell, the police, ICL, and local government. He has published widely on training issues, and in 1990 was appointed to the editorial advisory board of the *Journal of European Industrial Training*.

In the TRAINING ESSENTIALS series leading experts focus on the key issues in contemporary training. The books are thoroughly comprehensive, setting out the theoretical background while also providing practical guidance to meet the 'hands-on' needs of training practitioners. They are essential reading for trainers and for students working towards training qualifications – N/SVQs, and Diploma and Certificate courses in Training and Development.

Other titles in the series include:

Cultivating Self-development David Megginson and Vivien Whitaker

Delivering Training Suzy Siddons

Designing Training Alison Hardingham

Developing Learning Materials Jacqui Gough

Identifying Training Needs Tom Boydell and Malcolm Leary

Introduction to Training Penny Hackett

The Institute of Personnel and Development is the leading publisher of books and reports for personnel and training professionals and students and for all those concerned with the effective management and development of people at work. For full details of all our titles please telephone the Publishing Department on 0181 263 3387.

TRAINING ESSENTIALS

EVALUATING TRAINING

Peter Bramley

INSTITUTE OF PERSONNEL AND DEVELOPMENT

© Peter Bramley 1996

First published in 1996
Reprinted 1997

Design and typesetting by Paperweight
Printed in Great Britain by
The Cromwell Press, Wiltshire

British Library Cataloguing in Publication Data
A catalogue record for this book is available from the
British Library

ISBN
0-85292-636-7

**INSTITUTE OF PERSONNEL
AND DEVELOPMENT**

IPD House, Camp Road, London SW19 4UX
Tel.: 0181 971 9000   Fax: 0181 263 3333
Registered office as above. Registered Charity No. 1038333.
A company limited by guarantee. Registered in England No. 2931892.

Contents

Acknowledgement

Iwould like to express my thanks to Brenda Moran for her help during the preparation of this book. She read the draft and suggested many ways in which the ideas could be better expressed. The final product is a great improvement on the draft and much of this is due to her contribution.

1 Introduction

This book is written for those people directly involved in training – either as training specialists or as managers who have responsibility for training as a major part of their work. As such, they face demands from all sides for expertise in evaluation. Within organisations training managers are increasingly being asked to demonstrate the links between training activities and aspects of organisational effectiveness, while specific initiatives, such as 'Investors in People' or more general quality schemes, impose explicit requirements for assessing training and development plans and programmes. Staff development is only one organisational priority among many and must compete for scarce resources; it needs to be able to demonstrate its value in order to survive and prosper.

The aim of this book is to describe techniques which can be used for evaluating training activities. Some of them are simple techniques and some are not so simple. The intention is to describe these techniques and to provide practical advice on how they might be used. If the book is successful in meeting its aim it should be possible for those who wish to evaluate, but have no experience in doing so, to find techniques which they can use and which are appropriate for their purpose.

What is training?

We need a definition of the word 'training' to help us think about what we are to evaluate. Training involves learning, but it is rather more than that. Training implies learning to do something *and*, when it is successful, it results in things being done differently.

Much of what people learn during their lives is a result of unplanned experience. Although this can be powerful, it is not a very efficient way of learning. If what is to be learned can be described or specified then activities can be planned that will facilitate the learning by making it easier and quicker. Training should be like this: a planned process rather than an accidental one.

Within organisations, the investment in training is intended to result in increased effectiveness at work. The broad definition of training that is developed from these ideas, and that I want to use within this book, is

> A process which is planned to facilitate learning so that people can become more effective in carrying out aspects of their work.

This definition is chosen because it is broad enough to include activities such as on-the-job learning, team development, action learning and performance management as well as courses.

Models of training

The model of training that I prefer and that gives this book its structure is shown opposite in Figure 1.

This is a model for the design of training that meets our definition and seems appropriate for the times in which we live. Training is now treated as an investment that produces returns that can be related to the business plans of the organisation (one of the key questions in 'Investors in People'). This book will show how to build in evaluation at each stage of the design and delivery of training so that this can be achieved.

The book has been planned on the model shown in Figure 1. Chapter 2 will cover organisational effectiveness and

Figure 1

A MODEL OF TRAINING BASED UPON IMPROVING EFFECTIVENESS

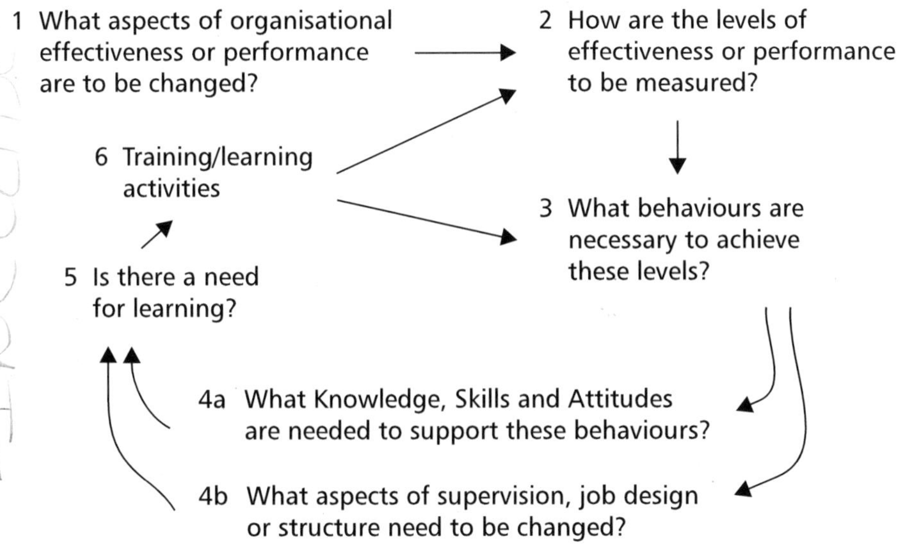

1 What aspects of organisational effectiveness or performance are to be changed?

2 How are the levels of effectiveness or performance to be measured?

6 Training/learning activities

3 What behaviours are necessary to achieve these levels?

5 Is there a need for learning?

4a What Knowledge, Skills and Attitudes are needed to support these behaviours?

4b What aspects of supervision, job design or structure need to be changed?

how to measure it (stages 1 and 2). Other chapters will describe how to measure changes in behaviour (stage 3), and how to assess learning (stage 4a). In Chapter 7 stages 4b and 5 will be discussed. The intention here is to assist with the decisions about how best to mix training with other organisational interventions in order to facilitate change. A description of methods of evaluating during a learning activity will be found in Chapter 8.

The use of a training model based upon increasing effectiveness in the organisational context is relatively new. A more traditional model of the training process, based upon individual learning in technical education, is shown in Figure 2 on page 4.

This model is suitable for educational activities carried out in classrooms, but I find it unhelpful when considering training in its broader sense. The problem is that it is a learning rather than a training model, and thus lends itself to evaluation at the learning rather than the application

Figure 2

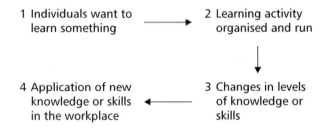

A MODEL OF TRAINING BASED UPON INDIVIDUAL EDUCATION

1 Individuals want to learn something ⟶ 2 Learning activity organised and run

4 Application of new knowledge or skills in the workplace ⟵ 3 Changes in levels of knowledge or skills

level. The model is suitable for training and testing off-the-job, but the application phase is usually left to the learner alone to accomplish. It is very difficult, when using this model, to carry out any evaluation of application of abilities in the workplace because the criteria for assessment are rarely specified in advance of the learning. Asking people afterwards whether they have been able to use the learning is a very poor substitute for evaluating against criteria of effectiveness.

What is evaluation?

Evaluation is a process of establishing the worth of something. The 'worth', which means the value, merit or excellence of the thing, is actually someone's opinion. This opinion is usually based upon information, comparisons and experience, and one might expect some consensus in this between informed people. Sometimes there is some disagreement about the worth of something because people are using different criteria to make the evaluation. For instance, some will attribute sentimental value to a piece of jewellery because of its association with a deceased relative, but find that the insurer's value is much lower. The process of evaluation thus provides information about the worth of something, but the decision whether to buy it, keep it, or whatever, may involve values other than those used by the evaluator.

Training could be involved in organisational change

Evaluation of training is a process of gathering information with which to make decisions about training activities. It is important that this is done carefully so that decisions can be based upon sound evidence. Good decisions to introduce, retain or discard particular training activities can make a major contribution to the well-being of the organisation; poor decisions are likely to be expensive. The decisions to be made will need to take into account a number of aspects of the organisational context and future organisational plans. The evaluation process is usually one of providing the decision-makers with information, rather than actually making the decisions.

The information gathered may satisfy a number of purposes. It might, for instance, be about the process of training, the changes attributable to it or increases in effectiveness of those who have undergone training. It might be to help to decide whether training is the most effective way of achieving some form of organisational change. It should be clear from this that it is necessary to identify the purpose of the evaluation before deciding what information needs to be collected. If this is not done the process of evaluation will lack focus and could become unnecessarily expensive. The aim of an evaluator should be to do a sound job with the resources available. It will never be possible to collect enough information to answer all possible questions.

Most of the purposes proposed for evaluation can be grouped under three headings:

Feedback   on the effectiveness of the training activities

Control   over the provision of training

Intervention   into the organisational processes that affect training.

Feedback

The most common reason for evaluating training is to provide quality control over the design and delivery of training activities. Feedback to trainers about the effectiveness of particular activities and the extent to which objectives are being met will help in the development of the programme being run and in the planning of future ones. What information is necessary for this purpose? You might require:

- some detail about the effectiveness of each learning situation and the extent to which it was suitable for its purpose
- before-and-after measures of levels of knowledge, skills, attitudes or behaviour
- some description of those for whom the activities were of most, and of least, benefit (to define the target population more closely)
- an assessment of the extent to which the objectives set for the programme (by the designers, the participants, the line managers, and the organisation) have been met. These objectives may be set at individual, team, departmental or organisational level.

Feedback evaluation will be of most benefit during the pilot stage of a new programme or when new activities are being introduced into older programmes. It may also be necessary if the target population of trainees changes.

Control

A second reason for evaluating training is to relate the training policy and practice to organisational goals. Decisions may need to be made about whether training is the best method of achieving changes. Usually training is not enough on its own and information about the best way of combining training with other organisational interventions is needed. Decisions may also need to be made about whether a particular set of training activities is worth sponsoring at all.

The information needed for control evaluation is:

Doesn't reflect well on the Company if the staff are badly trained.

- an estimate of the worth to the organisation of the output from the training activities
- an estimate of the cost of providing the activities
- a comparative study of different methods of solving the problem, different combinations of training with other actions such as improving performance management or re-allocating responsibilities
- a number of the items listed under Feedback (on page 6).

Control evaluation, if it is imposed upon the training department, may be seen as a threat by some trainers. My view would be that there are advantages in this type of evaluation because, if it is properly done, it highlights the contribution that training is making to the well-being of the organisation.

Intervention

The process of evaluation usually affects the views of people concerned with, or affected by, the training. That a training event is being evaluated will encourage some to think that its future is under review; others may think, 'It must be important, otherwise they wouldn't be spending money on evaluating it.' This can be used constructively by the sensitive evaluator to:

- encourage the supervisors and line managers to be more closely involved in pre- and post-briefing of participants
- change the ways in which participants are selected for learning activities so that a greater proportion of those attending are the right people at the right time
- encourage the co-operation of supervisors in the use of learning contracts and action plans to help integrate training into work procedures and thus ensure transfer of learning
- facilitate on-the-job activities which complement off-job training and thus foster continuous development.

Evaluation gives a legitimate reason for people from the training department to talk to managers about aspects of organisational effectiveness and how the training provision can assist in increasing this. It can assist in the liaison between trainers and the line. It can also provide information with which to make decisions about future training plans.

> Perhaps you might ask yourself what the purposes of evaluation in your organisation are? What kinds of evaluation are being carried out? Do they meet the purposes that you have identified?

Why evaluate training?

Some of the purposes of evaluation have been described above, but the broader question, 'Why evaluate training at all?' still needs answering. Over the past 10 years or so, interest in evaluation has intensified. The UK Government has required the evaluation of virtually everything in the public sector, under the banner of 'competitive tendering'. Some surveys of training provision have indicated that only about 10 per cent of the learning gained on off-the-job courses results in changes in effectiveness at work.[1] Can the organisation afford the investment in a wide range of activities that are not making any impact on effectiveness? How will decisions be made about which programmes should run and which should not? Evaluative information is necessary to support these decisions.

Some readers may belong to organisations that are attempting to become 'Investors in People'. Among the questions asked of applicants for membership are:

■ Have you established procedures for evaluating the effectiveness of training in relation to your business needs?

■ Are your line managers and trainees involved in evaluations?

▮ Assess levels of increased skills and knowledge: do your evaluations also record whether each trainee's performance on the job has improved?

It is clear that a comprehensive evaluation policy is necessary to provide the information necessary to answer these questions.

It used to be the case that the contribution of a training department was assessed by the number of days' training carried out during the year, and the value of the department was judged by the number of bids for places. Those days have gone, and with them most of the large training departments offering menus of courses. Now training departments, like other organisational functions, are required to demonstrate how they benefit the organisation. This requires a sophisticated system of evaluation.

There are, of course, costs incurred in evaluating. Sophisticated evaluation by trainers, managers or consultants takes up a great deal of expensive time. There are, however, clear benefits to be balanced against these costs. These include:

▮ improved quality of training activities
▮ improved ability of the trainers to relate inputs to outputs
▮ better discrimination of training activities between those that are worthy of support and those that should be dropped
▮ better integration of training offered and on-the-job development
▮ better co-operation between trainers and line managers in the development of staff
▮ evidence of the contribution that training and development activities are making to the organisation
▮ closer integration of training aims and organisational objectives.

Perhaps the question that we should be asking is not 'Why

evaluate training? but 'Can we afford not to evaluate training activities?'

Reference

1   GEORGENSON D.L. 'The problem of transfer calls for partnership.' *Training and Development Journal*, **36**(10) (1982) 75–78

2 Changes in Effectiveness

In this chapter I will try to show how to approach the description and measurement of aspects of effectiveness, stages 1 and 2 in our model of training. Detailed clarification of what training is trying to achieve in terms of increased effectiveness is the most difficult part of evaluation, and, in my experience, this is where most people need help.

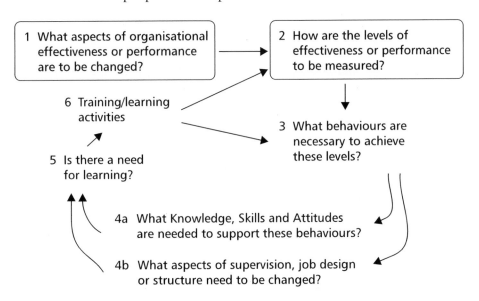

1 What aspects of organisational effectiveness or performance are to be changed?

2 How are the levels of effectiveness or performance to be measured?

6 Training/learning activities

3 What behaviours are necessary to achieve these levels?

5 Is there a need for learning?

4a What Knowledge, Skills and Attitudes are needed to support these behaviours?

4b What aspects of supervision, job design or structure need to be changed?

Before doing anything else in planning or evaluating training, it is necessary to sort out the expected impact that the activities will have on the effectiveness of the whole organisation, or specific parts of it. As with the identification of training needs, the analysis and measurement may be at organisational, team or individual level. What I am advocating is a detailed statement of how we intend to evaluate success, in performance measures of individuals, teams or divisions of an organisation *before* we plan or make any interventions that include training. This means building the criteria for evaluation into the training objectives.

To some this may seem strange. Many people think that objectives should be set before the event, but that this should be done in a fairly loose fashion to allow for variations in participant requirements. Evaluation is thought of as something that comes afterwards. Evaluation is then a process of asking participants whether the training helped them to achieve the (or their) objectives. My experience as an evaluator indicates that evaluation as an afterthought does not work at all well. If you do not decide how to measure the criteria of success before you start the intervention, the evaluation becomes merely a process of collecting a patchwork of opinions. These will have been affected by the training venue, the particular mix of people on the programme, and unrelated organisational changes, as well as by the training intervention itself. It is much more satisfactory to monitor criteria of effectiveness and assess whether things have improved as a result of the intervention.

In this chapter I am repeating, in broad terms, what other books in this series are advocating, that training policy should be closely linked to business plans, organisational objectives and priorities.[1] These should be used as ways of identifying what changes in effectiveness might be desired. When strategic decisions are made about what the organisation intends to be doing in five years' time, the implications for staff development should be considered. When training programmes are suggested, a detailed analysis should be made of their likely benefits to the organisation. How can it be done?

Impact analysis

One method of deciding what a programme or intervention should achieve, ie its purposes and how one might evaluate whether these have been achieved, is to carry out an impact analysis.

The starting-point of an impact analysis is a workshop in which the 'stakeholders' discuss the objectives for the programme and the behaviours that are likely to change as a result. The word 'stakeholder' refers to the people who have something to gain or lose from the proposed intervention. It will include the trainers who will produce, use or implement the programme, and also line managers who are expected to profit in some way from the programme, or who may be negatively affected. The intention is to involve a wide range of interested parties and thus get a comprehensive view of the proposed activities. Particularly important will be those who can, if they wish, make it difficult for any changes to take place.

Each of the stakeholders is asked to write down the three most important purposes for the programme. This should be done individually as these are likely to vary because of the different perspectives of the stakeholders. The 'purposes' can be written on slips of paper (Post-its) and pinned up on a board. The stakeholders are then asked to group the purposes into clusters and give each cluster a title. During this process it will often be necessary to clarify any statements of purpose that seem ambiguous. Each stakeholder then individually allocates 10 points across the clusters; adding up these scores leads to a ranking of importance of the clusters. The process thus produces a group view of the main purposes for the programme and a collective view of their relative importance.

The stakeholder group, assisted by the facilitator, then creates a forcefield by listing those events, people and factors that might help in achieving these purposes and those that might hinder. This part of the process is not essential, but it does help to clarify what the programme or intervention is intended to achieve.

The final stage is to agree criteria against which the success of the programme can be evaluated. These will, of course, be closely related to the purposes but may be either more general or more specific in tone. Sometimes the group will also identify which measures need to be taken before the intervention, to allow for later comparisons. The group may also decide to meet at some future date to review progress.

An example of such a workshop[2] is one which set the priorities, and means of evaluating them, when it was intended to introduce a number of courses on 'open systems' into a company that produces computer software. Because of the importance of these programmes, and the wide range of people who would attend them, many of the senior managers responsible for the various functions in the organisation were present at the workshop.

The key purposes that they set for the programme in order of priority are listed below. They were to:

1   enable the company to survive and prosper
2   close a skills gap and facilitate a speedy skills shift
3   establish a common language
4   create a desire for more knowledge of the subject
5   improve management decision-making
6   create a platform for better business usage of the skills
7   increase the extent to which people look outwards
8   enable individuals to innovate and influence within the company
9   improve the 'marketability' of individuals both internally and externally
10   maintain existing improvements.

The workshop participants discussed this list at some length and made many suggestions for impact measures. Some of these are listed below, and following each there is, in italics, a brief description of what was found during the evaluation one year later.

■ A positive percentage shift in particular business revenue and profit.

All units showed a positive movement in their revenue and profitability for 'open' products and services.

■ The figure for recruitment versus rationalisation costs; the resourcing of the skills internally; the potential marketability of technical staff.

There was a large reduction in numbers of technical staff with open systems skills who had to be recruited from outside. Staff were transferred to new divisions as planned; very few redundancies.

■ The introduction of new training events in the subject.

Eleven new courses introduced during 1993 and three dropped. Five new ones to be introduced in 1994 and eight dropped. Increase in requests for local delivery of short courses on 'open systems'. Demand for training constantly ahead of supply.

■ Sample key stakeholders and ask them to estimate which business opportunities they have been able to take advantage of as a direct result of having people trained in open systems skills.

The estimation was rather rough and ready, but came to over £10m; this for a training investment of £0.6m.

Aspects of organisational effectiveness

Another way to develop criteria against which to evaluate changes is to use a comprehensive framework for categorising organisational effectiveness. One that I have found very useful uses four major categories – achieving targets, attracting resources, satisfying interested parties, and internal processes.[3]

Achieving targets

The most widely used approach to effectiveness focuses on meeting goals and targets. Most organisations use basic measurements of work output to meet *product* goals. The emphasis may be on quality or quantity, variety, uniqueness or innovation, or whatever is the organisational focus. Types of indices that might be available are:

QUANTITY	QUALITY	VARIETY
units produced	defects/failure rate	diversity of product range
tasks completed	reject rates	rationalisation of product range
applications etc processed	error rates	product/service innovation
backlogs	rework	
turnover	scrap	
units sold	waste	
money collected	shortages	
on-time deliveries	accidents	

An example of increasing effectiveness, where this was defined as meeting goals, was provided by Allen and Hanburys.[4] Sales training was provided to coincide with the launch of *Serevent*, a treatment for asthma. Targets were set for the percentage of GPs who were aware of the product and the percentage who had prescribed it. The targets set for six months were achieved after only three months.

There are also *system* goals, which emphasise growth, profits, modes of functioning, return on investment etc. Possible criteria are:

■ productivity
■ processing time
■ profit
■ operating costs
■ running costs
■ performance/cost ratio
■ rates of achieving deadlines

∎ cost:income ratios

∎ on-time shipments

∎ percentage of quota achieved

∎ percentage of tasks incorrectly done

∎ efficiency

∎ levels of variation in the product or service

∎ ability to react to circumstances and cope with external pressures

∎ work stoppages

∎ time to reach job competency

∎ lead time for new products and services

∎ levels of supervision required

∎ amount of overtime

∎ lost time

∎ machine down-time

∎ frequency of accidents

∎ costs of accidents, breakdowns etc.

It might also be possible to look at increases in manpower, facilities, assets, sales etc compared with the organisation's own past state and that of its competitors.

An example of evaluating against system targets is given by one of the major building societies.[5] The cost:income ratio was well above the industry average and customer complaints had risen to a level that required a dedicated complaints department. Two-day workshops that covered process skills, developing staff input of ideas for quality improvement, and team problem-solving were provided for managers. The effectiveness of these workshops was monitored by system targets and, after one year, these were considered satisfactory. The cost:income ratio had fallen to the industry average and the level of complaints could be handled by normal line management.

Another example is provided by the TQM training programme for all employees, introduced by Pirelli Cables.

As a result of this, defect rates were reduced by up to 50 per cent and on-time deliveries improved from 90 per cent to 99.5 per cent.[6]

> What measures of 'product' or 'systems' goals are available in your own organisation? Are they being used to derive objectives for training programmes? Could they be used for this purpose?

Attracting resources

Looking at resources changes the emphasis from outputs, goals and targets, to inputs designed to achieve some competitive advantage. At the level of the organisation, the evaluation might be a comparison with major competitors or against 'how we did last year', or against some ideal desired state. At lower levels, increased flexibility is often the measure which is used. Criteria that might be chosen to assess increases in effectiveness include:

- increase in number of customers
- new branches opened
- new markets entered
- takeover of other organisations
- ability to change standard operating procedures when necessary
- ability to cope with external changes
- increase in the pool of trained staff
- skills for future job requirements developed
- increased flexibility in job deployment developed
- readiness to perform some task if asked to do so
- flexibility in meeting changing customer requirements
- improvements in the competence/skills pool.

The impact analysis described above offers an example of improving this kind of effectiveness. One of the criteria used was the number of technical staff recruited (and hence recruiting costs) and the redeployment of present staff (and thus very few redundancies). There are, no doubt, many examples in your own organisation, where increased flexibility of staff has resulted in greater efficiency and effectiveness.

Another example is that of Albion Pressed Metal. The flexibility of the workforce was increased by training, and this allowed the introduction of just-in-time manufacturing techniques. The result was a reduction in lead time from 10 weeks to five days, with associated financial benefits.[4] Hoover Ltd used the same type of solution to tackle a similar problem, and reported dramatic increases of 93 per cent in productivity and a reduction of 50 per cent in scrap.[7]

A recent survey of top UK chief executives (carried out by the Institute of Management) found that the primary reason for organisational change was not the recession but the need to improve competitiveness by reducing costs and increasing the flexibility of the workforce.

> Where is the pressure to improve flexibility in your organisation? What are the implications for training?

Satisfying interested parties

Effectiveness can be judged by the extent to which the organisation meets the expectations of groups whose co-operation is important. Assessment of effectiveness will be against criteria such as:

- customer complaints
- returned material
- repair orders on guarantee
- non-receipt of goods
- product or service quality
- awareness of customer problems
- company image surveys

- customer relations surveys
- recall costs
- incorrect goods received
- surveys within the organisation on employee satisfaction etc
- on-time deliveries.

Most organisations monitor criteria of this nature but few publish the information. I have already mentioned the case of the building society with a high level of customer complaints. Another example is that of Coin-a-Drink Ltd, which supplies automatic vending machines to workplace locations. Training was introduced to improve the efficiency of supply and this resulted in an increase in the customer satisfaction rating, as well as a decrease in the number of service calls which were needed to sort out on-site problems.[4]

Interested parties will also include those whose goodwill is necessary. For example, Short Brothers, who supply aircraft components to Boeing, were in danger of losing contracts because of late deliveries. Training was introduced to increase employee flexibility and on the use of total quality techniques, after which delivery schedules were met, the contracts were maintained, and Boeing's increased confidence led to new contracts for the supply of other products.[6]

> Who are the key 'interested parties' in your part of the organisation? What criteria are they using to evaluate the activities for which you are responsible? How do they gather the information with which to do this? Do you have any input into this evaluation?

Internal processes

Effective organisations may be defined as those in which there is little conflict within and between groups, where members feel satisfied with the system and where information flows smoothly. Assessment of effectiveness may be against hard data such as turnover of employees, absence, sick-leave etc, but often it is also against surveyed opinions of 'how we were' or 'how we would like to be'. The quality of internal processes can sometimes be assessed by attitude surveys on job satisfaction, group cohesiveness, or commitment.

Many survey instruments have been developed by consultants and researchers and useful examples of these inventories can be found in references (8), (9) and (10). Some examples are also included in Chapter 6 of this book, on measuring changes in attitudes. Improvements are usually monitored by comparing the percentages of employees who select the 'positive' boxes on scales such as: 'agree' or 'tend to agree', against those who choose the 'negative' end of the scale, such as 'tend to disagree' or 'disagree'. For instance, in one of the large building societies the 'positive' percentages to two of the 120 questions on the survey instrument changed as shown below.

	1993	1994
'In my judgement, company x as a whole is well managed'	34%	50%
'I would recommend company x as a good company to work for'	41%	51%

The intervention between the 1993 survey and that in 1994 was a series of two-day workshops for managers.[5]

Poor quality of internal processes may show in the statistics of:

transfer/turnover	disciplinary actions
absenteeism	grievances
medical visits	stoppages
accident rates	excessive work breakdown

If any are prevalent, they can be very expensive. Your

personnel department will be able to estimate the potential cost savings if the incidence of some of these can be reduced.

> Can you design a training activity for your organisation that might reduce the incidence of one of these? What would it cost? Would it be worthwhile in cost/benefit terms?

One way of doing this is to train specific employee groups in new skills and allow some enrichment of the job by increasing autonomy and variety. An example is given in Training Awards for Industry, 1993.[6] Dolland and Aitchison introduced training for receptionists in clinical and dispensing skills, with the intention of increasing job satisfaction and thus reducing turnover. After the training, the receptionists were regraded as 'optical assistants' and their turnover dropped from 60 to 21 per cent. The saving in recruitment costs was sufficient to pay for the training.

The London Borough of Havering introduced training for grounds maintenance staff so that they would have more confidence to face the future, which would include the challenge of competitive tendering. The reported results included lower staff turnover, decreased absenteeism and higher morale.[7]

I have found that using the four categories of effectiveness described above has been helpful when discussing with line managers exactly what is supposed to change as a result of a training programme, and how this change is to be measured. It is important, first of all, to establish what criteria the line managers are actually using to assess effectiveness and to identify by what criteria they themselves are being judged. The next stage is to identify the risks and related costs if these criteria are not achieved. Discussion of this leads to the identification of criteria against which to evaluate the contribution of training activities.

You might attempt some mapping of possible changes for courses already running using the four categories of organisational effectiveness. Try to identify the intended benefits from a course on something generic for individuals at a certain level in your organisation – say, principles of management for junior managers – and classify these into the four categories. Try to classify the intended benefits from a programme 'tailor-made' for improving the effectiveness of a particular individual or group at work. What criteria can you measure? What kind of programme do you find easier to evaluate?

Total quality management

Another very useful method for identifying criteria of organisational effectiveness is offered by the European model for total quality management (TQM). The nine areas that make up the definition of organisational effectiveness are:

▮ the enablers: leadership; people management; policy and strategy; resources and processes

▮ the results: people satisfaction; customer satisfaction; impact on society and business results.

Some detail on what is implied by seeking effectiveness in these nine areas is given in Table 1 on page 24. Further detail of the elements of the model are available from EFQM, and there is also an assessment pack for self-diagnosis.[11]

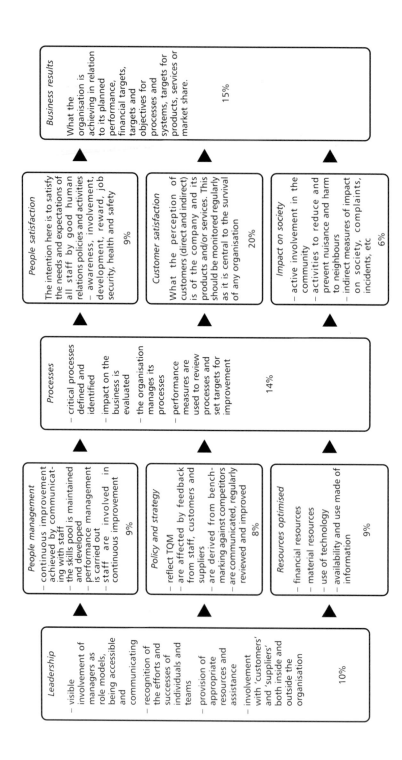

Leadership

– visible involvement of managers as role models, being accessible and communicating
– recognition of the efforts and successes of individuals and teams
– provision of appropriate resources and assistance
– involvement with 'customers' and 'suppliers' both inside and outside the organisation

10%

People management

– continuous improvement achieved by communicating with staff
– the skills pool is maintained and developed
– performance management is carried out
– staff are involved in continuous improvement

9%

Policy and strategy

– reflect TQM
– are affected by feedback from staff, customers and suppliers
– are derived from benchmarking against competitors
– are communicated, regularly reviewed and improved

8%

Resources optimised

– financial resources
– material resources
– use of technology
– availability and use made of information

9%

Processes

– critical processes defined and identified
– impact on the business is evaluated
– the organisation manages its processes
– performance measures are used to review processes and set targets for improvement

14%

People satisfaction

The intention here is to satisfy the needs and expectations of all staff by good human relations policies and activities – awareness, involvement, development, reward, job security, health and safety

9%

Customer satisfaction

What the perception of customers (direct and indirect) is of the company and its products and/or services. This should be monitored regularly as it is central to the survival of any organisation

20%

Impact on society

– active involvement in the community
– activities to reduce and prevent nuisance and harm to neighbours
– indirect measures of impact on society, complaints, incidents, etc

6%

Business results

What the organisation is achieving in relation to its planned performance, financial targets, targets and objectives for processes and systems, targets for products, services or market share.

15%

◄──── ENABLERS ────►   ◄──── RESULTS ────►

Table 1

THE EFQM (1994) MODEL OF ORGANISATIONAL EFFECTIVENESS

From our point of view, as evaluators, the model has great strengths. Most attempts at defining organisational effectiveness lead to measures in the 'results' area, some involve 'people satisfaction' and others 'customer satisfaction'. The ISO 9000 has 'processes' as its focus. The EFQM model includes all of these and also the 'enablers' without which the results cannot be achieved.

The process that I would recommend is to use the EFQM model to identify gains in effectiveness which are expected to result from a particular intervention. All nine areas are examined and questions asked about whether the activities will 'improve...', or 'fully utilise...' or 'cause appropriate staff to learn...'. The discussion generated by this will clarify exactly what the intervention is expected to achieve, set targets against which this can be evaluated, focus the design of the learning activities and identify organisational factors which need attention.

My experience with using this model suggests that if the intervention is to have a real and measurable impact, at least one area of 'enablers' and one area of 'results' should be included. Where the sponsors are arguing that the intervention will affect all nine areas, it may be so diffuse that the impact is lost because too wide a range of objectives is being set. Some of these objectives may be mutually incompatible, but even where this is not the case, changing all nine areas is an organisational transformation rather than the evolution and development of more effective ways of running the organisation.

The effectiveness of teams

It is possible to assess effectiveness at a team level rather than at the level of the organisation (or a department, or function, or section of it). If a team achieves the targets set for it, attracts the necessary resources, or provides products or services which satisfy interested parties, it could be said to be effective, and measures of *how* effective can be established. It is also quite common to assess the quality of the relationships within the group and how well it co-operates with other groups.

To be called a team, rather than just a group of people who work together, the group must have some common goals and problems. Interdependent action should be required to achieve the goals or solve the problems, and assessment of effectiveness should be based upon the activities of the team rather than on those of individuals. If the latter is the case, then it is more relevant to evaluate at the level of individual effectiveness (and reward on an individual rather than a team basis). For instance, a basketball team is a closely knit group which is highly interdependent, even though the individuals in it have different roles. The contribution of an individual is likely to be assessed in terms of how well he or she fitted in and co-operated with other members of the team. A Ryder Cup golf team is actually a set of 12 individuals. Most of the time they play independently, and their contribution is judged on how many points they contribute to the overall total. I would not include such a group in the definition of a team.

In work activities there seems to be an increasing tendency to group people into teams in the belief that this will lead to increased effectiveness. Where co-operation is necessary to achieve the desired outcomes this may be sound. The evidence suggests that shared processes, such as safety at work and customer care, become more effective through team development. It is also the case that teams can bring together a wide range of experience, which might be useful in giving different perspectives on the problem to be tackled. Perhaps the strongest argument in support of team working is that it is likely to increase participation when change is being discussed. Commitment to objectives, methods, tasks etc can often be enhanced by participation in discussion about targets and the means of achieving them.

On the other hand, there are many situations where teams are likely to achieve rather less than individuals. The classic study was carried out by a Frenchman towards the end of the last century. He asked students to pull as hard as they could on a rope and measured the strength of the pull. They did this individually and then in teams of seven. The average pull of a team of seven was 75 per cent of that of the aggregated individual members' pulls. This has been replicated in many different situations and is generally considered to be an example of 'social loafing', the widespread tendency for people to work less hard in groups than when they are solely responsible and accountable.

Many will argue that groups are more creative than individuals; the research evidence does not support this either. In experiments on 'brainstorming', where people are asked to generate as many ideas as they can in a given time (without evaluating whether the ideas are good, bad or silly), a group of five will usually produce about half as many ideas as five individuals in separate rooms. The quality of the ideas produced in the two situations is usually similar. This would suggest that the brainstorming should be done separately and then all of the ideas should be collected. The evaluation of the ideas and selection of those thought worthy of further examination would be better done in the group situation, because a range of views and experience would be valuable for this purpose.

Team effectiveness

The literature on team performance and development suggests that there are two main aspects of effectiveness: achieving the tasks set, and viability through consideration of the well-being of the team members. Some balance between these is necessary. Too much emphasis on the task can lead to longer-term problems with viability, as members are likely to opt out of a situation which ignores their well-being. Great emphasis on well-being can also be dysfunctional as it may lead to a 'cosy' group which spends its time looking inward and fails to fulfil the organisational purpose for which it exists.

Questions that an evaluator of team effectiveness might ask could include some of those listed below (many of the ideas here have been borrowed from the book by West.[12])

Achieving objectives

■ How clear are the objectives of the group?

■ How much agreement is there within the group about the objectives?

■ How realistic are the objectives thought to be?

■ What level of commitment to the objectives is there?

■ How concerned are team members with reaching high standards?

■ How often are the objectives reviewed?

■ What feedback on progress is given to the group?

■ How often does the team discuss methods of getting things done?

Well-being

■ Is everyone understood and accepted?

■ Is everyone listened to?

■ Do people support each other when things are difficult?

■ Is conflict brought out into the open and dealt with?

■ Do team members have good relationships with each other?

■ Is there support for new ideas?

■ Do team members help each other to develop?

The questions could be posed in interviews with the team members or printed as a questionnaire. For the latter purpose they might be rephrased as statements such as, 'The objectives for our team are clear to me' and the team members asked to 'agree/tend to agree/undecided/tend to disagree/disagree' with each.

Stakeholders' views on the effectiveness of teams

Another way to assess the effectiveness of a team is to collect the views of those individuals who have an interest in the work of the team. For instance, the important stakeholders may include those who receive goods or services, customers, general management, or leaders of other teams who have to co-operate with the team under consideration. The team members are also important stakeholders and their views must be considered if the team is to have any longer-term viability.

The opinions of these stakeholders on the team's effectiveness will reveal which criteria they are using to assess effectiveness and will thus provide items for measurement purposes. The framework suggested above (achieving targets, acquiring resources, satisfying constituents and internal processes) should help in this. A list of criteria generated from discussions with stakeholders can be produced and each can be assessed by members of the team. The questions to be asked of each item on this list are 'How important is this?' and 'How effective are we at this?'

Developing the effectiveness of teams

Team development activities may focus on working relationships or on action planning. There are three main models: problem-solving, interpersonal, and role-identification.

▌ When using a *problem-solving* model the team identifies problem areas (usually by 'brainstorming'). The areas of most importance are selected and actions are taken by individuals and the team to try to solve these problems.

▌ Where team development is undertaken using an *interpersonal* model, the intention is to increase the ability of the group to work together by emphasising the value of sharing, trust, and collaboration within the group.

■ The *role-identification* approach treats the group as a set of interacting roles and attempts to increase effectiveness through a better understanding and allocation of these roles.

It is, of course, possible to combine the different models, but I find that it helps to think in terms of each one separately when trying to identify criteria against which to evaluate increased effectiveness.

The problem-solving model

The most widely used example of the problem-solving model is found in 'quality circles' (QCs). Some years ago a survey was carried out of 86 companies in the UK which were supporting over 1,000 QCs.[13] Some 92 per cent of the companies claimed that their QC programme was successful.

Members of the circles thought that there were benefits. Increased job satisfaction, better teamwork within the department, recognition of their achievements and better relationships with management were cited. Management also thought that there were benefits, and the three considered most important were that first line supervisors were placed in a leadership role, that many problems were solved at grass roots level, thus allowing management to concentrate on higher priority items, and that it was possible to identify future managers among the QCs membership.

Overall the companies felt that the main benefits derived from the investment in QCs were:

■ increased involvement of employees
■ improvement in quality and productivity
■ a reduction of the barriers between management and shopfloor
■ improvement in communications across the company.

It seems likely that the effectiveness of problem-solving groups may be measured in terms of having led to significant cost savings, or having provided possible solutions to the problems identified. It may also be possible to calculate the value to the organisation of solving a particular problem. This might be done directly or by estimating how much consultant time has been saved. Often, team development aimed at improving problem-solving will also improve the quality of working life and feelings of well-being. This is a further worthwhile gain.

The interpersonal skills model

Interpersonal skills models are usually based upon the t-group approach, where the team sits in a circle and discusses how the members interact with one another. Often questions of trust, sharing, and communication of feelings are raised.

There is a good deal of published evidence that this kind of activity is likely to have some effect on attitudes – how one feels about others, the workplace, the value of the team, satisfaction with the work. This is the area of effectiveness that we have already seen above as 'internal processes', and I would argue that improvement in indices of these attitudes would be valuable in themselves as indicators of well-being at work. This is likely to contribute towards longer-term viability of the group, and it is also possible that improvements in it will be negatively associated with measures of stress, levels of sickness, absenteeism, and staff turnover.

Within this sort of approach it is possible to take measures of other things before, during, and after the developmental intervention. For instance, an increase in positive responses to some of the items which were listed under 'achieving objectives' on page 28 about the clarity of team objectives, the degree of information-sharing, commitment to excellence, and so on might well be taken as indicators of increased effectiveness.

There is little research evidence to suggest a reliable causal link between this kind of team-building and improved productivity or achievement of targets. You might think that increased satisfaction should lead to improved performance, but the evidence suggests a flow in the other direction; high performance tends to lead to the team's being more satisfied and more cohesive.[14]

The role-identification model

When a task group is formed to carry out an important project there is a tendency to select a few outstanding people who can contribute from specific experience and expertise. Such groups are often ineffective because all of the members want to offer ideas but few wish to work with ideas suggested by others. Within any group there should be people who try to get the work done – and done on time – as well as those who provide lots of good ideas. There should also be someone who is encouraging all members to contribute, and someone who is concerned about the objectives being set. The role-identification approach attempts to increase understanding of team roles such as these in the belief that this will enhance the contribution made by members.

Evaluation of the role-identification approach is difficult because the composition of each group is unique. It should be possible to assess increased awareness of roles, and thus increased openness and willingness to share work, on the part of the group members. However, the links with improved effectiveness in any of the four categories described above are not easy to predict.

What methods are being used in your organisation to increase the effectiveness of teams? How are improvements being monitored?

What measures are being taken?

A number of different measures have been suggested above; could any of them be used to monitor improvements in team performance?

The effectiveness of individuals

It is also possible to use stages 1 and 2 of our model of training to decide what changes in the effectiveness of individuals are desired and how these might be measured. Again, I would emphasise that the more specific the description of these changes, the more likely it is that training can be designed to achieve them.

Effectiveness is demonstrated in the work context by doing the right things at the right time. It is not just having the knowledge or the right attitudes, although these can clearly be significant contributors to effectiveness. We need to go further than learning and describe what we mean by effective behaviours.

Key results areas

One way of defining effectiveness in a job is to identify the key results areas. Most jobs have a lot of day-to-day routine activities that need to be done but have no great impact on whether the job-holder is doing the job well. Key results areas usually represent only a few of the tasks in the job, but they are those that are crucial.

There are many ways of identifying key results areas, but all require some focusing down to isolate the few really important aspects of the job. One method is to list all of the tasks which might be done and then ask the job-holders and supervisors to agree on the 10 per cent that are crucial to success. Another is to start with a long list of possible competence areas, define the job in terms of those that are relevant and then select from this shorter list (the job definition) the 10 that are the key to achievement of the current job objectives. In both of these approaches it helps if job-holders and supervisors carry out the analysis separately and then, through discussion, agree the key results areas. More information on how this might be done is included in *Identifying Training Needs*,[15] which is part of this *Training Essentials* series.

A well-known attempt to list the key results areas for supervisors is:

- orienting a new employee
- giving on-the-job training
- motivating a poor performer
- conducting a performance review
- handling discrimination complaints.[16]

For each area it is necessary to describe the behaviours which are expected to lead to successful performance. For instance, with 'motivating a poor performer', these might be:

- Focus on the problem, not on the personality.
- Ask for his or her help and discuss his or her ideas on how to solve the problem.
- Come to an agreement on what each of you will do.
- Plan a specific follow-up date.

Another way of identifying key results areas is to analyse what it is that people are doing who do the job well, and contrast this with the behaviours of people who do not do the job so well. A useful technique here is the Repertory Grid (described on pp 66–73). For instance, 'rep-grid' analysis was used to identify what behaviours were expected from good middle managers (actually section leaders) in an oil company. They were:

- joint target-setting and reviews of progress
- holding team meetings to discuss priorities
- accepting responsibility but delegating authority
- asking for views before making decisions
- discussing development opportunities with subordinates
- coaching and guiding rather than telling.

The best people to comment on whether managers actually do these things are their subordinates, and further detail on how this information might be collected is given in the next chapter (p 43).

Some may be wondering if there is a difference between what I am calling key results areas and the more general concept of competence. I think that there is. I am not talking about a list of generic competence areas which are required for adequate performance of a job, and which all job-holders will need. These would be provided by some generic training which would be evaluated on attendance, learning, and day-to-day on-the-job performance. The focus of 'key results' analysis is specific competence areas for particular individuals that can be improved by some version of just-in-time training, and which will have a marked impact on performance.

Individual effectiveness might also be judged by the extent to which targets are achieved. Where action learning is being used, or work-based projects, the achievement of the goals can be related, as a benefit, to the cost of providing the learning opportunities. Learning contracts offer similar possibilities for evaluating against goals, but care is needed to ensure that these lead to increased effectiveness. Where the assessment of the achievement of targets is a rather imprecise appraisal at the end of a year, the process will rarely offer a sufficiently precise focus for evaluation of training activities during the year.

In brief

Effectiveness is not a simple concept: there are many ways of categorising it, many views on which particular aspects are important, and many methods of defining the criteria of interest. The ones that I have found to be most useful are:

At the *organisational* level:

∎ impact analysis by senior managers

∎ the four categories of achieving goals, attracting

resources, satisfying interested parties and internal processes

■ a total quality model.

At the *team* level:

■ achieving objectives
■ feelings of well-being
■ stakeholders' views
■ a focus on process issues (we will return to this in the next chapter).

At the *individual* level:

■ key results areas.

Many techniques for identifying criteria of effectiveness have been described, but there is also a major underlying theme that (I hope) has been clearly stated. It is that, although it may be difficult to define and measure the criteria of effectiveness which are of interest, it is important to do so.

The criteria that are expected to show an improvement after the training activities need to be identified *before* the learning situations are designed. The activities can then be designed specifically to achieve the desired changes, and it will be possible to incorporate any necessary changes in the job context and thus facilitate transfer of the learning. It will also be possible to set up an evaluative framework to discover whether the expected changes have actually been achieved. Trying, as an afterthought, some weeks after the training, to identify criteria against which to evaluate is a very poor substitute.

References

1 BOYDELL T. and M. LEARY *Identifying Training Needs*. London, IPD. (1996)

2 BRAMLEY P. and B. KITSON 'Evaluating against business criteria.' *Journal of European Industrial*

Training, **18**, 1, (1994) 10–14

3   Developed from CAMERON K. 'Critical questions in assessing organizational effectiveness.' *Organizational Dynamics.* (Autumn 1980.) 66–80. More fully described in BRAMLEY P. *Evaluating Effective Training* (2nd Ed) Maidenhead, McGraw-Hill. (1996)

4   *National Training Awards* 1991, Room W823, Sheffield S1 4PQ, Employment Department

5   BRAMLEY P. *et al.* 'Evaluating effective management learning.' *Journal of European Industrial Training,* MCB Press. (1996)

6   *National Training Awards* 1993, Room W823, Sheffield S1 4PQ, Employment Department

7   *National Training Awards* 1992, Room W823, Sheffield S1 4PQ, Employment Department

8   HENERSON M.E., L.L.MORRIS and C.T. FITZGIBBON *How to Measure Attitudes.* Beverley Hills, Sage. (1978)

9   COOK J.D., S.J.HEPWORTH, T.D.WALL and P.B.WARR *The Experience of Work.* London, Academic Press. (1981)

10 SEASHORE S.E., E.E. LAWLER, P.H. MIRVIS and C. CAMMAN *Assessing Organizational Change.* New York, John Wiley & Sons. (1982)

11 EFQM *Total Quality Management: The European model for self-appraisal.* The European Foundation for Quality Management, Avenue des Pleiades 19, 1200 Brussels, Belgium, Tel: (32) 2775 3511. (1995)

12 WEST M.A. *Effective Teamwork.* London, Routledge. (1994)

13 DALE B.G. and T.S. BALL *A Study of Quality Circles in UK Manufacturing Organizations.* Department of Management Sciences, UMIST, Manchester. (1983)

14 MULLEN B. and C. COOPER 'The relation between group cohesiveness and performance: an integration.' *Psychological Bulletin,* 115, (1994) 210-227

15 BOYDELL T. and M. LEARY *Identifying Training Needs*. London, IPD. (1996)

16 GOLDSTEIN A.P. and M. SORCHER *Changing Supervisor Behaviour*. New York, Pergamon Press. (1974)

3 Changes in Behaviour

In this chapter we will examine stage 3 of the training model, attempting to answer the question, 'What behaviours are necessary to achieve increased effectiveness?' Doing this implies being able to:

▪ label the behaviours and thus distinguish them from others

▪ measure the frequency or quality of the actions that are of interest

▪ establish the links with some form of effectiveness.

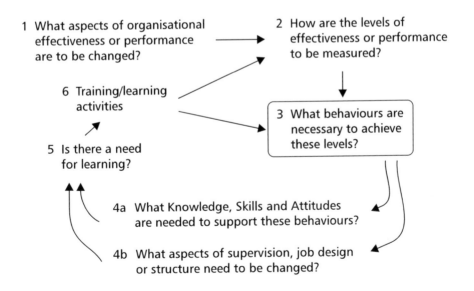

1 What aspects of organisational effectiveness or performance are to be changed?

2 How are the levels of effectiveness or performance to be measured?

6 Training/learning activities

3 What behaviours are necessary to achieve these levels?

5 Is there a need for learning?

4a What Knowledge, Skills and Attitudes are needed to support these behaviours?

4b What aspects of supervision, job design or structure need to be changed?

Using a competence approach

Probably the best-known method of linking behaviours to effectiveness is to list the competence areas associated with success. The list may be derived from interviews with, or from check-lists filled in by, those who do the work and their managers. Training needs can then be established by assessing individuals against this list of competence areas. Developmental opportunities, on or off the job, should then be provided in areas of perceived weakness. The training activities necessary to achieve this would subsequently be evaluated in terms of whether the learner and his or her manager felt that performance in the area was no longer weak.

The areas of competence required will vary from job to job. The assessment of whether or not there is still weak performance in a particular area can only be made against the requirements of the particular job. Some organisations appear to be attempting assessment of ability according to a set of competence areas, all of which are required to reach some absolute standard. Chasing high standards in everything, whether or not this is needed, can be very costly, in terms of both time and money.

A good example of the competence approach is given by the Management Charter Initiative (MCI) description of personal competence for managers.[1] There are four clusters within this – planning, managing others, managing oneself and using intellect – and each cluster is broken down into dimensions and behaviours. The framework is given in Table 2 on page 41.

For each dimension there are a number of behaviour indicators. For instance, for 'Showing concern for excellence' these are:

- Establish and communicate high expectations of performance. (This includes setting an example to others.)
- Actively seek to do things better.

Table 2

THE MCI PERSONAL COMPETENCE MODEL

CLUSTERS	DIMENSIONS
1 Planning to optimise the achievement of results	1.1 Showing concern for excellence
	1.2 Setting and prioritising objectives
	1.3 Monitoring and responding to actual against planned activities
2 Managing others to optimise results	2.1 Showing sensitivity to the needs of others
	2.2 Relating to others
	2.3 Obtaining the commitment of others
	2.4 Presenting oneself positively to others
3 Managing oneself to optimise results	3.1 Showing self-confidence and personal drive
	3.2 Managing personal emotions and stress
	3.3 Managing personal learning and development
4 Using intellect to optimise results	4.1 Collecting and organising information
	4.2 Identifying and applying concepts
	4.3 Taking decisions

▮ Continually strive to identify and minimise barriers to excellence.

▮ Use change as an opportunity for improvement.

For 'Showing sensitivity to the needs of others' the indicators are:

▮ Make time to be available to support others.

▮ Reinforce others' self-worth and value in what they do.

▮ Demonstrate patience and tolerance when others are expressing themselves or encountering difficulties.

- Demonstrate acceptance of others' holding different views.
- Encourage others to express themselves honestly.
- Actively seek to identify and clarify the attitudes, views and feelings of others.

Evaluation will take place by assessing the frequency and appropriateness of use of these behaviour indicators. Measures before and after will indicate whether there has been a change, and if this is in the desired direction.

The strength of this approach is that it breaks down the competence areas into behaviours that can be monitored by the learner, the supervisor, direct reports and colleagues. It is thus possible to communicate whether there have been changes in the desired direction or not.

I would contrast this with the more usual method of using competence areas within annual performance appraisal schemes. The most common areas are oral communication, leadership, judgement, initiative, organising, written communication, motivation and analytical skills.[2] The job holder is usually judged on areas such as these against a scale of something like 'High/Exceeds/Fulfils/Below' or 'Strong/ Adequate/Weak'. These categories are too general and too poorly defined to provide criteria against which to evaluate changes in behaviour and effectiveness due to learning. If this is to be attempted, competence areas should be broken down into the specific behaviours that are to be used to make the judgements.

For example, for 'communication' one might use a set of behaviours such as the following:

- takes time to listen and understand the situation
- chooses the right time to communicate
- chooses the right medium and style for communication
- is assertive and communicates when necessary
- shows sensitivity to the positions and feelings of others.

For 'motivation', a possible set of behaviours might be:

■ shows enthusiasm when problems arise
■ sees opportunities rather than difficulties
■ sets high standards and goes for them
■ welcomes responsibility and challenge
■ persists when others might give up
■ high energy level, can handle a large volume of work.

Using behaviour scales

These lists of desirable actions suggest a second method of linking behaviours to effectiveness – the use of behaviour scales.

Suppose, for example, that we want to change the management style in our organisation to a more consultative one. We would need to focus on the behaviours consistent with a more consultative style. For instance, we might try to increase the frequency of doing things such as target-setting and discussing priorities, asking for views before making decisions and delegating authority.

One way of doing this is to define, by listing examples of relevant behaviour, what is meant by the desired approach and then assess to what extent this is being achieved. The people best able to carry out this assessment of middle managers are the junior managers who report to them. Some intervention would then be made, based upon feeding back the subordinates' views to the middle managers and then offering opportunities to attend workshops on skills that they wished to develop. A possible set of such behaviours is:

■ communicates company objectives to you
■ jointly sets clear targets with you
■ jointly reviews progress on targets at timely intervals
■ lets you know exactly what is expected of you
■ delegates sufficient authority and responsibility to you

- accepts full responsibility for your actions even when things go wrong
- encourages you to suggest new ideas on how things could be done
- asks for and uses your input in decision-making
- expresses appreciation personally when you do well
- shows genuine interest in you and your work
- demonstrates concern about your development
- coaches and guides effectively
- is available and spends time with you when needed
- encourages good relationships among his or her staff
- knows when individuals have problems, is helpful and supportive.[3]

The subordinates would be asked to apply each of the 15 statements to the behaviour of their own departmental head and mark each statement 'agree = 1', or 'tend to agree = 2' and so on, to 'disagree = 5'. This is best be done in a way that allows subordinates to give their views anonymously. The opinions should be collated and used for individual feedback to the managers whose behaviour is being reviewed. The departmental heads thus learn of their subordinates' views on their management styles, discuss these (with a consultant or with each other) and agree an action plan or learning contract. Opport-unities to attend short workshops on joint target-setting, holding team meetings and developing subordinates would be offered. Six months or a year later, the process would be repeated and differences noted.

Changes in opinion about specific behaviours are of primary interest, and these can be related to the actions undertaken by the departmental heads. It is also possible, by collating all of the results, to gain some information on whether the style within the organisation has changed. For instance, in Table 3, the percentages of subordinates choosing the opinions 'agree = 1' to 'disagree = 5' are shown for years one and two of the feedback process.

Table 3

COMPARISON OF YEAR1/YEAR2 PERCENTAGES (PERCENTAGES BASED ON N = 194/193)

	Agree				Disagree
	1	2	3	4	5
Communicates company objectives	5/26	28/40	43/24	18/7	6/3
Jointly sets targets	10/29	33/43	32/18	23/10	2/0
Jointly reviews progress	9/15	22/34	34/21	32/30	3/0
Lets you know what is expected	13/20	37/46	20/22	27/12	3/0
Delegates sufficient authority	28/45	42/37	16/15	7/3	7/0

The percentages for the first year, on the left in Table 3, show that the perceived style was not at all consultative. Less than 50 per cent of the subordinates 'agree' or 'tend to agree' (ie chose ratings 1 or 2) with most of the statements. The percentages in year two are closer to those desired, but still show substantial proportions of subordinates who 'disagree' or 'tend to disagree' (ie chose the ratings 4 or 5).

The behaviours which showed most change in this study were procedural changes – setting up more team meetings, routine discussion of priorities and progress, putting in place development reviews and so on. Behaviours which were more closely related to personality traits – accepting full responsibility, encouraging new ideas and so on – showed less change.

The Royal Mail also uses this kind of approach to changing management behaviour. Information is collected from employees by using a set of 30 questions about the behaviour of their team leader. The list of questions has six sections – vision, commitment, approach to people, approach to business performance, personal contribution of manager, and communication – which reflect a view of what constitutes effective management behaviour in that particular organisation. In cycle 1, the subordinates are asked whether their team leader performs in ways such as those listed in Table 4 (some of these are abbreviated). These anonymous ratings are collated by the team leader who considers them and then attends a workshop with a group of colleagues. During the workshop issues are discussed and clarified and options for improvement considered. An outline improvement plan is developed and the leader then meets with his or her team to discuss the implications and actions to be taken. The whole procedure is repeated in six months (cycle 2).

Statistics are available for ratings by 8,470 team members on the 1,645 team leaders who have been through the two cycles.[4] A sample of the questions and the percentages associated with the choices made by subordinates is shown in Table 4.

In all of the questions there is a shift to the positive responses of between two and eight per cent. Given the number of people involved (8,470), these are worthwhile gains. The biggest changes are in questions 2, 12, 15, 17 and 18. As with our earlier example, these items, in the main, reflect changes in procedures. The smallest changes are in questions 13, 23, 24 and 27 and again one sees that these items are largely associated with personal styles and personality variables.

Another way of assessing changes by using behaviour scales is shown in Table 5. The categories chosen would, of course, reflect the definition of 'positive management' appropriate to the particular organisation. The perceived frequencies of present use of these behaviours could be assessed by the learner, and objectives set for increased use of some of them. Such behaviour scales also lend themselves to '360 degree appraisal' by seeking the opinions of the supervisor, colleagues and subordinates, as well as those of the developing manager. Differences in perception between the manager and the rest of the set are of particular interest, and these tend to highlight the

Table 4

TEAM MEMBERS' RATINGS OF LEADERSHIP BEHAVIOUR

The leader of your team	Disagree 1 & 2	Agree 3	Agree strongly 4
1 provides a clear and exciting vision	32/26	55/57	13/17
2 communicates how the vision translates into stretching goals	34/27	53/57	13/18
7 involves the team when making decisions	36/30	45/48	19/22
12 supports personal development and training	25/18	49/50	26/32
13 encourages and values personal feedback	26/22	49/51	25/27
15 encourages new ideas and suggestions	32/15	50/51	27/34
17 sets high work standards	16/11	51/49	33/40
18 encourages continuous improvements	20/13	53/54	27/33
23 displays integrity and a caring attitude	23/21	48/50	29/29
24 walks the job and is approachable	24/21	45/47	31/32
27 often speaks with the team	22/18	47/47	31/35
28 asks for ideas and listens	27/21	48/51	25/28

Where: 1=disagree strongly, 2=disagree, 3=agree, 4=agree strongly, 0=not enough evidence to mark

difference between believing and actually doing something that reflects that belief. This is a common problem in management development, because creating the right attitude does not always result in changes in behaviour in the workplace. We will look at this in more detail later, when we discuss measuring changes in attitudes.

Table 5

A BEHAVIOUR SCALE FOR POSITIVE MANAGEMENT

Positive management	Never 0–19	Seldom 20–39	Sometimes 40–59	Generally 60–79	Always 80–100%
Thinks ahead and develops plans rather than constantly clearing up problems	( )	( )	( )	( )	( )
Grasps the essential nature of the problem, knows what information is necessary and where/how to get it	( )	( )	( )	( )	( )
Thinks in terms of objectives rather than vague generalisations, and makes them both clear and realistic	( )	( )	( )	( )	( )
Takes decisions rather than procrastinating or passing problems up to the next level	( )	( )	( )	( )	( )
Is concerned about, and effective in, obtaining high productivity in the short and longer term	( )	( )	( )	( )	( )
Acts as a model for the group, being firm, getting commitment and encouraging participation	( )	( )	( )	( )	( )
Co-ordinates the group's activities and checks on progress to achieve objectives	( )	( )	( )	( )	( )
Deals with subordinates as individuals and makes each accountable for a specific set of responsibilities	( )	( )	( )	( )	( )
Knows what to delegate and has the courage to risk errors by subordinates	( )	( )	( )	( )	( )
Minimises immediate pressure and problems, and maximises long-term productivity	( )	( )	( )	( )	( )
Sets high standards and gets them	( )	( )	( )	( )	( )
Knows what is wanted and how to get it without resentment	( )	( )	( )	( )	( )
Seeks increased value for money and year-on-year improvements in efficiency	( )	( )	( )	( )	( )
Rewards outstanding performance	( )	( )	( )	( )	( )
Makes opportunities to develop people as individuals	( )	( )	( )	( )	( )

Categorising interpersonal skills

In some situations, where the cluster of behaviours is not well defined, the first problem is being able to describe and label the behaviours which are of interest. One of the first (and still one of the best) sets of categories for doing this is that of Rackham and Morgan.[5] The 13 categories were developed from research on interpersonal skills training, and are:

Proposing behaviour that puts forward a new concept, suggestion or course of action (and is actionable).

Building behaviour that extends or develops a proposal which has been made by another person (and is actionable).

Supporting behaviour that involves a conscious and direct declaration of support or agreement with another person or his concepts.

Disagreeing behaviour that involves a conscious, direct and reasoned declaration of difference of opinion, or criticism of another person's concepts.

Testing understanding behaviour that seeks to establish whether or not an earlier contribution has been understood.

Summarising behaviour that restates in a compact form the content of previous discussions or considerations.

Seeking information behaviour that seeks facts, opinions or clarification from another individual or individuals.

Giving information behaviour that offers facts, opinions or clarification to other individuals.

Shutting-out behaviour that excludes, or attempts to exclude, another group member (eg interrupting, talking over someone).

Bringing-in behaviour that is a direct and positive attempt to involve another group member.

Defending/attacking behaviour that attacks another

person or defensively strengthens an individual's own position. Defending/attacking behaviours usually involve overt value judgements and often contain emotional overtones.

Blocking/difficulty stating behaviour that places a difficulty or block in the path of a proposal or concept without offering any alternative proposal and without offering a reasoned statement of disagreement. Blocking/difficulty stating behaviour therefore tends to be rather bald; eg 'It won't work', or 'We couldn't possibly accept that'.

Open behaviour that exposes the individual who makes it to risk or loss of status. Included in this category would be admissions of mistakes or inadequacies, provided that these are not made in a defensive manner.

The 13 categories are used to track the frequency of use of the behaviours that are of interest. Important categories are selected by observing the behaviour of those thought to be good, and by contrasting the frequencies used by them with those used by people thought to be less good. For example, people who are rated as being good at appraisal interviewing:

■ ask more questions, particularly to request proposals or solutions from the person being appraised
■ test understanding more often
■ summarise more often
■ make fewer proposals themselves.

Another example is that of people who are helping customers choose flights for holidays or business trips. One might expect:

a high rate of:
■ seeking information
■ testing understanding
■ building
■ summarising.

a lower rate of:

■ proposing
■ giving information
■ bringing in.

no:

■ blocking/difficulty stating
■ defending/attacking
■ shutting out.

The 13 categories listed can be used for on-the-job development by observation and feedback, or for off-the-job courses on interpersonal skills. Their main benefit is that they provide labels so that behaviours of interest can be classified, measured and changed. As we shall see, the first stage in any skills training is to learn the names of the parts. Without this knowledge, communication about what is required for effective work is very difficult.

Behaviour in groups

A good deal of team development work is based upon the view that improving the processes that groups use to work together will increase effectiveness. For example, having observed a group working together, the facilitator might ask them questions such as:

■ How clear was the purpose of the task? If it was not absolutely clear, why did you not ask about it?

■ Who set the objectives for the meeting? To what extent were these shared?

■ Who put in the ideas? Who had ideas that they did not put in? What use was made of creative ideas?

■ What actions helped the team? What actions hindered the team?

■ How were differences of opinion or difficult issues handled?

The attention is then focused on the processes which are being employed, and how effective these are in using the abilities of all members of the team. A useful process model to help with this assessment has been suggested by Schein.[6] The framework for the analysis, and some of the questions to ask, are given below.

	TASK	INTERPERSONAL
CONTENT	1 Formal agenda, goals	4 Who is doing what to whom
PROCESS	2 How the task is done	5 How members relate to each other, communicate etc
STRUCTURE	3 Recurrent processes, 'standard operating procedures'	6 Recurrent interpersonal relationships, roles

Box 1   Why is the group there? What is its task? What are the goals of the meeting?

Box 2   Do they listen, misunderstand, interrupt? Do they spend time on trivial issues, or have side conversations? How is the group chaired? How are decisions made?

Box 3   What procedures are used? Who is allowed to interrupt whom? Have members of the group got particular roles or tasks?

Box 4   Who tries to dominate and control, who argues, who supports whom, who interrupts whom? Who initiates, who checks consensus and who summarises?

Box 5   Do they build on each other or vie for attention? Do they confront each other or are they polite? Is someone persistently attacking someone else?

Box 6   Have they developed a special, common language? Is there a marked 'informal' structure? Are there implicit rules of behaviour? Is there an informal reward system? Are there rituals and procedures for unpredictable events?

The evaluator will note activity in each of these boxes, and the key question to consider in each case is, 'Which of these events are most relevant to increasing the effectiveness of the group?' Feedback to the group and discussion with them should provide some answers to this question.

Schein also suggests a number of key activities for facilitators of groups:

- clarify the purpose of the meeting
- insist on openness
- encourage new approaches
- encourage activity:
  - what I hear you saying is…
  - to summarise, what you mean is…
  - could you headline that last point so that we can record it?
  - could you say some more about that?
  - what does the rest of the group think?
  - what ideas do people have to add (or to build) on that?
- focus on the useful and relevant
- manage digressions and interruptions
- seek contributions from as many people as possible
- good time-management
- paraphrase for understanding
- ensure that key themes are recorded.

This list of activities can quite easily be converted into a check-list with which to observe what a team leader does. Concrete feedback on performance can be provided by ticks and crosses against each of these items, with a few well-chosen examples to support the opinions. One of the key aspects of team effectiveness is how the team leader behaves and this observation of process in team meetings offers valuable information on this.

In brief

In this chapter I have tried to show how measures of behaviour can be used in evaluation. In all of the examples the link with effectiveness in the work role has been emphasised. Changing behaviour is not easy, and if it does not result in increased effectiveness the feedback will be unhelpful, and the new ways of doing things are likely to be rejected. A model which is worth considering is shown in Figure 3. A much more complex and complete version of this relapse process is given in Marx.[7]

Figure 3

POSITIVE AND NEGATIVE LINKS BETWEEN BEHAVIOUR AND EFFECTIVENESS

Effective behaviour is usually context-dependent: actions which are successful in some situations are not so in others. The strength of using a competence approach is enhanced when the competence areas identified are those that can be demonstrated in the work setting and are associated with doing the job well. Such categories are ideal for use in evaluating changes due to training interventions. The use of broad, general areas of competence does not provide useful criteria for such purposes.

In assessing whether changes in behaviour have taken place, the opinions of subordinates are particularly valuable. Such information is not often available to managers and the feedback which it provides can be a powerful stimulus for change.

Behaviour scales need unambiguous, shared definitions. These can only be established by thorough research. It will usually be necessary to spend some time isolating, defining and labelling the behaviours of interest and then establishing that they have a direct link with effectiveness.

Measures of frequency or quality, taken before and after the training activities, will be necessary to establish that desired changes have taken place.

References

1   *MCI Pocket Directory, Middle Management Standards.* London, Management Charter Initiative.

2   HIRSCH W. and S. BEVAN *What Makes a Manager? In Search of a Language for Management Skills.* University of Sussex, Institute of Manpower Studies. (1988)

3   BRAMLEY P. 'Using Subordinate Appraisals as Feedback'. Paper given to the 23rd International Congress of Applied Psychology, Madrid. Copies available from the Department of Organizational Psychology, Birkbeck College, University of London. (1994)

4   BRAMLEY P. *et al.* 'Evaluating effective management learning,' *Journal of European Industrial Training,* MCB Press (1996)

5   RACKHAM N. and T. MORGAN *Behavioural Analysis in Training*. Maidenhead, McGraw-Hill. (1977)

6   SCHEIN E.H. *Process Consultation Volume II*. Reading, Massachusetts, Addison Wesley OD Series. (1987)

7   MARX R.D. 'Relapse prevention for managerial training', *Academy of Management Review*, 7, (1982) 27-40

4 Evaluation of Learning: Changes in Knowledge

In this chapter, and the two that follow, techniques for measuring learning will be described and discussed. In our model of training this represents stage 4a: 'What knowledge, skills and attitudes are needed to support these behaviours?'

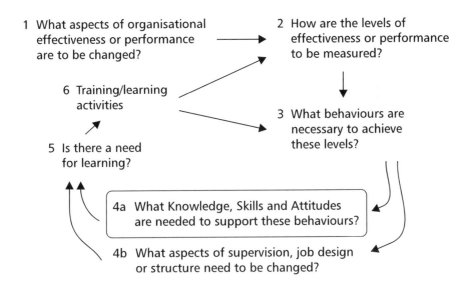

1 What aspects of organisational effectiveness or performance are to be changed?

2 How are the levels of effectiveness or performance to be measured?

6 Training/learning activities

3 What behaviours are necessary to achieve these levels?

5 Is there a need for learning?

4a What Knowledge, Skills and Attitudes are needed to support these behaviours?

4b What aspects of supervision, job design or structure need to be changed?

There is an interesting debate about when learning can be said to have taken place. Some psychologists would argue that learning is a relatively permanent change in behaviour, and thus that learning in an organisational context can be demonstrated only by changes in the ways in which work activities are carried out. Others would argue that learning takes place when people begin to think differently. Learning can then be an end in itself, regardless of whether it results in different work behaviours. The debate is interesting because it forces us to think about the underlying model of training. The model based upon individual education (Figure 2) has, as its third stage, 'changes in levels of knowledge or skills', and the fourth stage, whether or not these are applied, remains an assumption. When using this model, training would be evaluated by assessing whether learning has taken place. Training as a process of increasing effectiveness (the model shown above and in Figure 1), assumes that learning is required to produce changes in work behaviour. A more appropriate level at which to evaluate learning would thus be that of assessing changes in behaviour.

Whichever model is being used, it is possible to specify what learning is required for satisfactory job performance, to measure the level before a training activity and again afterwards, and thus evaluate whether the expected learning has taken place. Learning is a 'whole person' activity and it has knowledge, skills and attitudinal components, but to achieve some clarity in presentation, techniques for measuring aspects of learning will be described in the three following chapters.

Changes in knowledge

Almost all of the tasks within a job require the job-holder to have some knowledge. One aspect of designing a training activity would, therefore, be to

- discover what knowledge is required for satisfactory job performance
- discover what trainees know when they start the training
- plan how best to facilitate the closing of this gap.

A method of clarifying what knowledge is required that I have found valuable is to carry out an analysis at three levels of complexity:[1]

Level 1, facts: the basic requirement for knowing facts, rules and lists.

Level 2, procedures: knowledge of procedures, how things are done, how to order sets of actions.

Level 3, analysis: being able to recognise the key features in particular situations and thus select the most appropriate procedure from a number of possibilities.

The levels are built on each other in increasing complexity, and the training should be designed to move up the levels. The training needs analysis will be at all three levels to facilitate this design process. The evaluation might be at any level but will usually be a demonstration of ability at levels two or three.

Testing knowledge is common in technical education, in trades and when candidates apply for membership of professional bodies. Those who do not have the required level of knowledge are deemed not to be able to do the work. This ought also to apply to in-company training, but often it does not. This is usually because the analysis of needs has not been done in sufficient detail to justify statements such as, 'The level of knowledge which X has shown implies that he should not be given work of type W'. There is, of course, a great deal of sensitivity about testing ability, particularly that of managers, and one needs to be on firm ground in order to make such statements.

Measuring knowledge

Open-ended questions which require short answers may be posed to assess knowledge of facts, lists and procedures. They can also be used to test powers of analysis. The answer expected should be short, and a clear statement should be given of how

Road signs that are triangles with red borders are warning signs.

True/False

With this type of item it is necessary to avoid the use of words like 'never' or 'always' in the stem, because these are usually false statements and thus offer help in identifying the correct answer.

It is clear that if a person who knows nothing is faced with a true/false test, he or she should score about 50 per cent by guessing at each item. A guessing correction can be applied to calculate the actual level of knowledge:

True score = Number of items correct – Number of items wrong

With multichoice items there is less likelihood of guessing in a random fashion. If necessary, guessing can be reduced by instructing the candidates not to guess but leave questions unanswered when they have no idea what the answer is. It is also possible to use a guessing correction, with the formula now becoming:

$$\text{True score} = \text{Number right} - \frac{\text{Number wrong}}{(\text{Number of alternatives} - 1)}$$

For instance, a candidate has 75 right, 15 wrong and has not attempted 10 on a multichoice test with four alternatives.

$$\text{True score} = 75 - \frac{15}{(4-1)}$$

$$= 75 - 5 \qquad \text{True score} = 70$$

As the candidate has not attempted 10 of the questions, can one say that he or she guessed the answers to the 15 which are wrong and five which are right? I think probably not; it seems more likely that the candidate had some idea about these answers: otherwise he or she would not have attempted them. The amount of guessing which is occurring can, in itself, be an interesting measure of knowledge. Someone who has learned something should not need to guess when answering questions.

Early evaluations of the effectiveness of teaching were based upon test results but they still have something to offer to evaluators of training. For instance, the mean (average) mark will tell us how difficult the trainees found the test to be and thus whether further training is necessary. It is also possible to compare the effectiveness of two different methods of training by comparing test results. However, the use of test results to help with decision-making implies that the test is a reliable measuring instrument. This will need to be established with any test, and a simple way of estimating reliability is described in the Appendix. Further information can be found in reference (2).

Gains in knowledge

If it is intended to attribute changes in levels of knowledge to training it would appear to be logical to measure knowledge before, as well as after, training and thus estimate the gain. Testing only afterwards is risky, as it may be that some of the participants actually knew more before training than they do afterwards. You think that a ridiculous statement? Well, I know of an occasion when it happened. I was asked to help with the evaluation of a knowledge-based programme – the learning of product-knowledge to support sales of particular products. The information to be learned was nicely packaged and all of the sales staff were expected to work through the packages and complete the knowledge tests. I suggested that they should be pre-tested as well as post-tested, and this was done. We found that some of the experienced sales staff scored higher marks on the pre-test than on the post-test! They had been either confused or bored by the learning packages.

Quite often, pre-testing is a waste of everyone's time as the learners can be considered to know very little, and they can safely be given a pre-test score of zero. Sometimes

and understanding in order to estimate how they are organising the knowledge which they have. For example, asking them how they make decisions about which procedures are more likely to succeed; asking them about what sub-goals they have for the procedures, and how these are linked to the overall goal of solving the problem.

Sometimes the concepts which people have are confused, and it is necessary to find out how they are thinking about the topic by carrying out an analysis of their 'mental maps'. A useful method for this analysis is the 'repertory grid'. Using this technique, the investigator asks the learner to consider a number of situations and to say what criteria he or she would use to distinguish between them, usually to distinguish those that went well from those that did not. This is often done in interviews but it can be done with groups and, for our purposes in evaluation, the group method will usually be more practical and less time-consuming. An example of the group method should help to clarify the procedure.

Suppose you are planning a programme for junior managers on 'communication'. A good starting-point would be to try to discover what they think good communication skills are. It should then be possible to plan the programme to start from this baseline and, by building on this, move their views closer to those which are thought to be valuable within the organisation.

You start by asking the participants to write down the names of six managers with whom they have worked, two who are thought to be very good communicators, two who are thought to be poor, and two who are in between. Each participant does this independently. No attempt is made by the tutors to explain what they mean by good communication skills. The intention is to find out what the participants think. Each name is then written on to a separate piece of paper; these are shuffled and then coded A, B, C, D, E, and F.

You now ask the participants to select A, B, and C from

the six and think about what each of these three managers might do in work situations where they are required to communicate. What is it that two of them might do that is similar? What is that one might do that the other two would probably not? Each of the participants selects a pair, from the three labelled A, B, and C, who are likely to behave in a similar way and a single who would behave quite differently. Each then writes down the pair description on the left of a prepared form, as below.

Triad Selection

Pair Description	A	B	C	D	E	F	Single Description
Try to make sure that I understand	✦	✦	✦				Too busy, just tells me

Quite often these are obviously opposite statements, but this is not always the case.

Next they draw the managers D, E, and F from the six and repeat the process of deciding what two of them would do that makes their behaviour alike and what the other one would do that would be different. For instance:

Selection

Pair Description	A	B	C	D	E	F	Single Description
Listen to what I have to say				✦	✦	✦	Not interested in my views

It is important to supervise this and ensure that the descriptions written down are about what managers *do* rather than descriptions of personality. Quite often the trainees will want to write down things such as 'warm personality', but such statements are at too high a level of generality to help us decide what needs to be learned in order to demonstrate 'warmth'.

what, for each of them, is the definition of good communication skills. With a group these contrasts can be collected and written up on flipcharts. This provides an interesting way to introduce the programme.

For example, at the beginning of a five-day programme of trainer training, one of our groups produced a list which included the following:

Most effective trainers	Least effective trainers
Confident in subject	Not interested
Ability to simplify	Inability to simplify
Can use different styles	Simply teaches
Outgoing	Laborious
Pitches talk at audience	Arrogant
Clarity of communication	Difficult to understand
Well-prepared	Disorganised

Some personality descriptions have slipped in here and these contrasts need further expansion. What was meant by 'outgoing', and what behaviour would be classified as 'arrogant'? These are questions that would need to be asked. Discussing types of behaviour in this way gives a good lead into talking about what good trainers do, and thus into the main topic of the programme.

This group procedure takes about one and a half hours, but it gives a good feel for the understanding that the participants have at the beginning of the programme. It is also a good introduction to the area as it requires them to think carefully about the subject and clarifies what they as individuals believe.

Towards the end of the training the procedure can be repeated and the results compared. As they will now be familiar with the process, the second attempt will take much less time – perhaps 45 minutes. Changes can be assessed in a number of ways:

■ More contrasts scoring zero or two or 16 or 18. At the beginning many of them will have only a few such contrasts as their views about the topic are likely to be rather woolly. At the end they should be much more focused on the area which has been discussed.

■ There should be fewer personality traits and more descriptions of what people do.

■ The constructs being used at the end should be influenced by what has been included in the programme.

The evaluation of a course for sales staff offers an example of a before-and-after analysis of constructs.[3] At the beginning of the training, the delegates produced constructs such as the following:

Effective sale reps	*Less effective sales reps*
Good sales records – get results	Do not turn in good results
Highly self-confident	Less assertive
Ambitious	Unimpressive
Set clear objectives	Play things by ear

Towards the end of the programme, their understanding had changed and they were thinking more about behaviours than about personalities. They produced contrasts such as:

Effective sales reps	*Less effective sales reps*
Listen as much as they talk	Talk far more than they listen
Modify their behaviour in interaction	Stick rigidly to a predetermined plan
Use a genuine problem-solving approach	Use an 'I am here to sell you something' approach
Use a range of different approaches/styles	Fixed characteristic style

In brief

The level of knowledge which people have is relatively easy to assess. Measurement at level 1, 'facts', can be carried out by using open-ended, short-answer questions or objective tests. The latter are used more often than the former because they allow more questions to be asked in a given time, and thus a wider coverage of the knowledge.

Measurement at level 2, 'procedures', can be carried out using objective test items but is more often done with open-ended, short-answer questions. Listing the steps, or 'What would you do next?' questions require the learner to *recall* the knowledge, whereas objective test items often prompt the learner by offering a set of alternatives from which the correct answer is to be *recognised*.

Measurement at level 3, 'analysis', often involves asking the learners about their mental maps, how they are making decisions about what to look for, how they decide what to do next, and so on. The repertory grid can be useful in clarifying some aspects of this because it requires the identification of the contrasts which are being used to make judgements.

Knowledge tests are not so widely used as one might imagine. They are common where it is necessary to demonstrate that professional standards have been reached. They are also common in packaged instructional material which is based upon the format of 'test then learn then retest'. This self-appraisal of level of knowledge is good learning design as it provides clear goals for the learning and feedback on performance. Goal-setting helps with both direction and persistence of learning[5] and is thus a useful motivator.

References

1   BLOOM B.S. (Ed.) *Taxonomy of Educational Objectives*. London, Longmans. (1956)

2   BRAMLEY P. *Evaluating Training Effectiveness* (2nd Edn) Maidenhead, McGraw-Hill. (1996)

3   HONEY P. 'The repertory grid in action'. *Industrial and Commercial Training*. (September 1979)

4   NISSIM R.E. 'The Fostering Process'. Unpublished Doctoral Thesis. University of Reading. (1996)

5   LOCK E.A. and G.P. LATHAM *A Theory of Goal-setting and Task Performance*. Englewood Cliffs NJ, Prentice-Hall. (1990)

complete concentration to press down the clutch, change gear and pull away smoothly. Eventually, it must be possible to do this automatically, so that some attention can be concentrated on the conditions of the road and traffic movements. This 'skill automaticity' is required in many tasks so that attention can be given to making decisions rather than being glued to the detail of the process.

Testing skills

Skills should generally be tested by practical tests. Sometimes it is possible to assess the skill by asking the candidate to state the correct sequence of actions. However, listing the sequence is not the same as actually performing the task. I can explain to someone how to set the make/break contacts in the distributor on my old tractor, but when I try to *do* it I never seem to get the setting right.

Tests of skills fall into two main types:

■ The trainee is set a task (for example, to repair something) and the work is inspected at the end of the test period.
■ The trainee is watched throughout the test so that the methods used can be assessed.

Inspecting finished work is a more economical use of the tester's time than watching the whole process but, if the actual procedure used is important, it may be necessary to spend the time doing this. Some kinds of repaired articles, for instance welded pieces of metal, may not reveal the quality of the repair from a simple surface inspection.

Where long procedures are being tested, watching the whole process allows the possibility of correcting the trainees who make mistakes early. They may then carry on with the test rather than stop and have the possibility of showing that they understand other parts of the procedure.

Research into the use of assessment centres has shown that practical tests are better predictors of job success than knowledge tests. This is probably because they more accurately simulate the job tasks for which people are being trained. Practical tests do however have some disadvantages:

- They are expensive to supervise.
- They may involve the use of expensive equipment.
- It is often difficult to screen candidates so that they cannot see what others are doing.

They can also be unreliable if a detailed marking guide is not used. Just how serious this can be is demonstrated by a simple exercise using electrical three-pin plugs. Six plugs are wired up to three-core cable, with one wired correctly and the others with defects, say:

a wired correctly	*d* wrong lead to earth
b live lead to neutral	*e* loose cable retainer bar
c too much bare wire	*f* one loose connection

Ask a number of people to mark the work (and give them no further information). Usually people will mark the wired plugs out of 10 and some give quite high marks for work that is actually dangerous. In later discussion, it can be established that some aspects of the work are critical because they involve safety. Then it becomes obvious that candidates who ignore safety aspects must fail. The general point being made here is that, where more than one marker is being used, some standardisation of the marking guide will be necessary to ensure reliability of testing. A guide will also be needed for the observation of performance tests. Standard driving test schedules are made up of lists of critical skills, each to be performed to a satisfactory level. For other performance tests it might be possible to video-record a number of attempts and, from these recordings, agree a marking schedule. Figure 4 overleaf shows a simple schedule (for marking attempts to change a car wheel) that was developed by this method.

With skills training there is often an assumption that the learners know very little and that pre-testing is, therefore, inappropriate. This is not always the case; sometimes pre-testing will show that the training programme needs to be modified to meet different target populations, some of whom know nothing and some needing only a little extra training.

One method of doing this is to use a 'trainability test'.[1] The essential components of the skill to be learned are analysed and then tasks are constructed that will incorporate some of these. The tasks must:

- be based upon crucial elements of the job
- use only such skills as can be learned during a brief learning period
- be sufficiently complicated to allow a range of observable errors to be made
- be capable of being carried out within a reasonable time.

A trained tester, normally an instructor who is experienced in the job, demonstrates what has to be done, or briefly teaches what has to be learned. The applicant then tries to complete the task under test conditions while observed by the tester. A record is kept of errors made during this part of the process.

A trainability test of this type was used in the selection of applicants for the job of machinist.[2] The candidates were graded on the test as:

A = extremely good – would expect her to become a very good machinist in a short time

B = fairly good – would expect her to reach 100 per cent performance in a reasonable time

C = good enough for simple work – would expect her to become a steady worker on a simple machine or task

D = would have difficulty in training

E = would not be trainable.

The great strength of this procedure is that it assists in the redeployment and training of staff at a time when some skills are becoming obsolete and new skills need to be learned. This is now a common experience, and it is worth while trying to avoid the costs of losing good staff and the recruiting costs of replacing them. Training costs can be reduced by establishing that the proposed trainees can easily learn the necessary skills. It is also the case that realistic job samples allow the potential trainees to make an appraisal of whether they actually wish to do that kind of work; motivation is always an important aspect of learning.

Another reason for pre-testing is to try to 'tailor' the programme to those who need training. I was once asked to help with the training of fitters to carry out the servicing of central heating systems in homes. An off-job programme of three one-week modules was designed to cover the skills necessary to carry out the work. All the fitters were tested using fault-finding exercises mounted on boards which represented the main types of heating system. The ways in which the fitters attempted these simple diagnostic tests were used to decide how many of the one-week modules each should attend. It was then possible to plan a programme of training courses which accurately met the skills needs across the population of fitters. Really efficient training is made possible by assessing the starting level of the trainees and then offering just-in-time learning.

Profiling skills

Profiling is widely used in education as a method of recording the development of students. In technical education the best known example is that of City and Guilds of London Institute who use a format of five attainment levels, each of them defined. For instance, the levels for 'planning' are:

Table 9

A FOLLOW-UP QUESTIONNAIRE FOR SUPERVISORS

Tasks	Is it necessary for him or her to do this?		Can he or she do it to your satisfaction?			Would you rather have trained him or her to do this yourself?	
The trainee has been taught to:	Yes	No	*Yes, without supervision*	*Yes, with supervision*	*No*	Yes	No
diagnose mechanical faults in							
repair or assist in the repair of							
use							
supervise someone using							
etc . . .							

It may be necessary to interview a sample of participants and their managers to discuss details of why things are difficult or why some performances are not up to standard. This might be done direct or by telephone.

In brief

The testing of skills has been common practice for a very long time. The classic model for skills learning is:

▪ The instructor demonstrates the whole task.

▪ The instructor breaks down the task into stages and demonstrates these one by one.

▪ Learners practice the stages one by one.

▪ Learners connect the stages to carry out the whole task.

▪ Learners are tested for proficiency.

The testing can be carried out relatively informally but, if it is to be reliable, quite detailed marking schedules may be needed. These should include critical aspects which need to be carried out correctly or safely if the performance is to be judged satisfactory.

An important aspect of the evaluation of skills training is the assessment of whether the skill is actually necessary for successful job performance. It is also worth considering whether the learning of the necessary skills is best done on or off the job. Key criteria to help with this decision might be:

▮ the availability of on-the-job supervision and coaching
▮ the time needed to achieve proficient performance
▮ the possible risk to people and equipment of on-the-job training
▮ the cost of off-the-job training.

Some of the skills needed by managers might be assessed in the ways described above or by testing their knowledge. However, most of their learning is intended to change the way in which they do things in the work context, and it is usually more informative to assess the learning at the behavioural level. As we have seen, it is also possible to assess their learning by some measurement of the effectiveness of the team section or department for which they are responsible.

References

1   Downs S. *Trainability Testing: A practical approach to selection training*. Information Paper no ii. London, HMSO. (1977)

2   Downs S., R.M. Farr and L. Colbeck 'Self-appraisal: A convergence of selection and guidance.' *Journal of Occupational Psychology*, **51**, (1978) 271-278

attention because it has been shown to be a good predictor of performance.[2] It is measured by asking for self-assessments of confidence to do particular tasks. For instance, one reported study asked for assessment of self-efficacy before training by using the following:

'Operating this PC as a word processor involves turning the machine on, calling up a WordPerfect program, inserting a diskette and calling up the relevant file.' I am capable of doing this when...

	Can do yes/no	If yes, confidence on a scale of 1 to 10 (not at all – totally)
I am provided with written instructional material	_____	_____
I am able to listen to someone giving instructions who pauses as I complete each step	_____	_____
I am able to watch someone going through the steps before I try it myself	_____	_____
there is an instructor to guide me by telling me each step as I proceed	_____	_____

Another reported example involved the measurement of confidence to do particular aspects of the job of first line manager before, during, and after an outdoor activity programme.[3] The managers were asked:

'How would you rate your confidence to carry out the following tasks and be successful in doing so' (Not at all confident = 1, Absolutely confident = 10)

Tasks such as the following were used:

Motivate and encourage staff to achieve goals   _____

Monitor the performance of staff   _____

Make decisions on work-related issues   _____

The measures used showed an improvement in the managers' self-efficacy after the programme, particularly for those who were low at the beginning. Some of this increased confidence was transferred to the work situation and resulted in greater effectiveness.

Semantic differentials

A simple way of measuring attitudes, and thus monitoring changes, is to use pairs of antonyms, words that have opposite meanings. At the beginning of the workshop the participants are asked to think about a particular topic and to express their view on it using seven-point scales. For example, one that I have found useful when running workshops on 'evaluating training' is shown in Table 10.

Table 10

A SEMANTIC DIFFERENTIAL

Evaluation of training is:

valuable	1	2	3	4	5	6	7	worthless
sincere	1	2	3	4	5	6	7	insincere
relevant	1	2	3	4	5	6	7	irrelevant
objective	1	2	3	4	5	6	7	subjective
fair	1	2	3	4	5	6	7	unfair
fast	1	2	3	4	5	6	7	slow

The opinions of the group can be summarised at the beginning of the workshop as frequencies on each line by counting those choosing a particular number. Some discussion then takes place about why the numbers have been chosen and this starts to identify attitudes to the topic. The exercise can be repeated near the end of the programme and any changes in attitude can be identified. It should be possible from this to assess whether positive changes have occurred on the dimensions of interest.

Other pairs of words which might be suitable for other topics are:

good–bad   friendly–unfriendly
strong–weak   interesting–boring
clear–confusing   profound–superficial
open–closed   relaxed–tense
useful–useless

It is, of course, possible to be more specific about the contrasts in which you are interested. For instance, with a workshop on evaluating training, you might start with opposites, such as those in Table 11.

Table 11

VIEWS ON THE PROCESS OF EVALUATION

Evaluation of training *should* be:

	1	2	3	4	5	6	7	
statistical and scientific, as its primary concern is with objective measurement	1	2	3	4	5	6	7	anecdotal and descriptive, as its primary concern is with subjective interpretation
a carefully planned process with a set agenda	1	2	3	4	5	6	7	changing throughout as the focus changes during the process
estimating the value of training activities to the organisation	1	2	3	4	5	6	7	providing feedback to the training department
based on large samples and asking quite simple questions	1	2	3	4	5	6	7	based on small samples and using in-depth questioning
part of the process for all training activities	1	2	3	4	5	6	7	carried out only when there is some doubt about a programme

(Adapted from an idea by Len Gill of Merseyside Police)

The questions represent important issues which need to be discussed and resolved within the workshop. The process of filling in, and then discussing, such an attitude measure raises awareness of these issues and starts the attitude changes that seem to be necessary.

Attitude surveys

Surveys of opinions on issues thought to be important to the effectiveness of the organisation have already been mentioned in Chapter 2, where we considered 'internal processes' as one method of assessing effectiveness. Such surveys are used by many organisations to monitor year-on-year changes in the attitudes of employees, and some of the items can be used to provide information for the evaluation of training activities.

Two types of format are widely used. One is based upon antonyms such as those above, and an example is shown in Table 12.

Please fill in the inventory below by circling the number which you think best describes your view of the organisation.

Table 12

AN EXAMPLE OF A FORMAT FOR AN ATTITUDE SURVEY

The management:

is task-centred and impersonal	1 2 3 4 5 6 7	is people-centred and caring
is cold, formal and reserved	1 2 3 4 5 6 7	is warm, informal and friendly
emphasises conserving resources	1 2 3 4 5 6 7	emphasises developing and using resources

Decisions are:

made by 'legal mechanisms'	1 2 3 4 5 6 7	made by problem-solving
treated as final	1 2 3 4 5 6 7	can be altered as circumstances require
made at the top	1 2 3 4 5 6 7	made at the lowest possible level

It should be possible to use opinions such as those in Table 12 to monitor changes in attitudes of employees. To some extent these could be affected by the introduction of management workshops on 'team development', 'delegating authority and responsibility' and so on. They could also be affected by other changes in the work situation which have nothing to do with training; for instance, changes in rates of pay or decisions on 'downsizing' the organisation.

Another way of laying out an attitude survey of this type is to label the statements 'x' and 'y' and ask whether the respondents agree with one or the other. An example of this is shown in Table 13.

Table 13

AN ALTERNATIVE LAYOUT FOR ASSESSING ATTITUDES USING PAIRED STATEMENTS

(*AX*=Agree X, *TAX*=Tend to agree X, *U*=Uncertain, *TAY*=Tend to agree Y, *AY*=agree Y)

Statement X	AX	TAX	U	TAY	AY	Statement Y
Communication in this organisation passes down, top to bottom						Communication flows across and upwards, as well as down
People hide what they really think and feel						People tend to express what they think and feel

An alternative format which is often used in attitudes surveys is to offer only one statement and then ask whether or not the respondents agree with it. An example is given in Table 14 opposite.

Some use 'strongly agree/agree' and 'disagree/strongly disagree' rather than 'agree/ tend to agree' but I think this is simply a matter of preference. Some designers of attitude surveys wish to force an opinion by not including an 'uncertain' column. I am dubious of the value of this. I have found that my main interest has been in the strength of 'positive' responses of TA and A or the 'negative'

Table 14

AN ALTERNATIVE FORMAT FOR AN ATTITUDE SURVEY USING SINGLE STATEMENTS

(D = disagree, T = tend to disagree, U = uncertain, TA = tend to agree, A = agree)

	D	TD	U	TA	A
When developing a new policy, 'away days' are held so that all interested parties can discuss the issues	1	2	3	4	5
Action plans from performance appraisal discussions influence the development of policies	1	2	3	4	5
When there is conflict you can expect a way forward to be imposed from above	5	4	3	2	1
The management develops policies, we are informed of the details and are expected to implement them	5	4	3	2	1
Policies are strongly influenced by interested parties outside the organisation	1	2	3	4	5
When there is conflict you can expect differences to be aired and support in finding a way forward	1	2	3	4	5

responses on TD and D. The use of an undecided column helps in the assessment of this. If your decision is to use only four columns, I would suggest that you use a fifth column which is labelled 'no evidence on which to make a judgement', to avoid artificially forcing an opinion from your respondents.

Some of the statements in Table 14 should attract positive responses and some negatives ones. The scoring of 12345 has been reversed (54321) to accommodate this. I find this reversing of questions, some positive and some negative, helps to avoid the respondents just ticking quickly down the list of questions. The reversals make them stop and think about each question before answering it.

There are others ways of laying out such an attitude survey, depending upon the information which is of interest. A fairly common format requests estimates of frequency, with such choices as:

1	Often		1	Almost always
2	Fairly often		2	Often
3	Occasionally		3	Occasionally
4	Once in a while		4	Seldom
5	Very seldom		5	Almost never

Another format seeks opinions on relative importance with dimensions such as:

1	Unimportant		1	Yes, to a great extent
2	Of little importance		2	Yes, to some extent
3	Rather important		3	Neither yes nor no
4	Very important		4	No, not particularly
5	Absolutely essential		5	No, definitely not

Describing survey results

With each of these formats a set of frequencies will be calculated to represent the opinions given. These may be published as raw figures if the numbers are small, but it is better to convert them to percentages where the numbers are large. Whether a number is 'large' is, to some extent, a matter of judgement. Reporting results is intended to inform people, and the nature of the audience must be considered. My view would be that for total responses fewer than 50 the raw frequencies will give more information; above 50 it becomes less likely that the raw figures will be easily understood.

For instance, in the example below the actual numbers are useful because changes in individual perceptions during the programme would be of interest:

The evaluation of training is:

a carefully planned process with a set agenda	1	0	4	6	2	0	1	changing throughout as the focus changes during the process

On the other hand, in an organisation-wide survey the clarity may be enhanced by conversion of the raw figures to percentages as these are easier to understand. For example, in a survey of subordinates' views of their managers' styles, the following raw figures were obtained from 194 respondents:

Your supervisor:	A	TA	U	TD	D
delegates sufficient authority and responsibility to you	54	81	31	14	14

I think that these figures are easier to understand and discuss when expressed as percentages; indeed, many people will start converting them roughly in their heads or on pieces of paper to improve their understanding. In this case the conversion is fairly simple

Your supervisor:	A	TA	U	TD	D
delegates sufficient authority and responsibility to you	28	42	16	7	7

It is, of course, important to state in the table of results of the survey what the size of the population of respondents was. In this case the statement would be, 'Percentages based on 194 responses to the 203 questionnaires distributed.' It is also important that the respondents are representative of the part of the organisation being surveyed. This may mean either a high proportion or a very carefully selected sample.

In brief

Attitudes are not as easy to measure as levels of knowledge or skills. They may, however, be equally important in predicting performance levels. It may thus be worth while assessing attitudes even when the main aim is an increase in knowledge or skills.

Self-efficacy, the perception that a particular situation or task can be handled successfully, seems to be a particularly good predictor of future performance. This is probably because it is associated with willingness to try something, and with persistence in the face of difficulty. Training events should be designed to develop this attitude and evaluated in terms of how successful they have been in doing so.

Attitude surveys are one way of assessing the 'internal processes' aspects of organisational effectiveness. These measures can be affected by events which have nothing to do with training. However, it is possible to include in such surveys specific questions that can measure changes in attitudes likely to be affected by management behaviour, and thus provide evidence on the effectiveness of management development activities.

There is an extensive literature on measuring attitudes, and it has not been possible to discuss it in any depth within this book. Interested readers who would like further information on employee surveys are referred to the book by Walters.[4] Those who are more interested in measuring individual attitudes should find reference (5) useful.

References

1   BANDURA A. *Social Foundations of Thought and Action*. Englewood Cliffs, N.J. Prentice-Hall. (1986)

2   GIST M.E., C. SCHWORER and B. Rosen 'Effects of alternative training methods on self-efficacy and performance in computer software training.' *Journal of Applied Psychology*, 74,6, (1989) 884-891

3   DONNISON P.A. 'The Effect of Outdoor Management Development on Self-efficacy'. Unpublished MSc dissertation, Birkbeck College, University of London. (1993)

4   WALTERS M. *Employee Attitude and Opinion Surveys*. London, IPD. (1996)

5   HENERSON M.E., L.L.MORRIS and C.T. FITZGIBBON *How to Measure Attitudes*. Beverly Hills, Sage. (1978)

7

Evaluation before Designing a Learning Event

Evaluating *before* the event may sound like an odd idea to those who are more familiar with evaluation at the end of the training cycle. However, very few training events are planned, designed and run if it is not thought likely that they will result in some worthwhile learning. Someone, usually the training manager, has carried out an evaluation in the sense of judging its enhancement value, as part of the decision to run the programme. If this evaluation is to be more than just an opinion, some estimate will need to be made of the expected benefit and the likely cost of the activities. A number of ways this pre-evaluation can be done are discussed in this chapter.

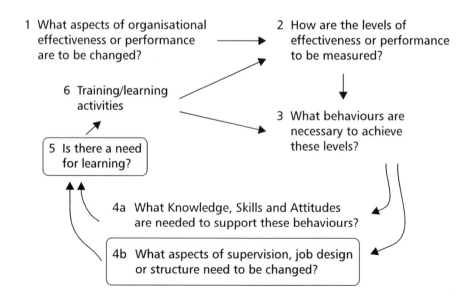

1 What aspects of organisational effectiveness or performance are to be changed?

2 How are the levels of effectiveness or performance to be measured?

6 Training/learning activities

3 What behaviours are necessary to achieve these levels?

5 Is there a need for learning?

4a What Knowledge, Skills and Attitudes are needed to support these behaviours?

4b What aspects of supervision, job design or structure need to be changed?

Stage 5 of the model is a pre-evaluation of how likely it is that a training activity will be the best way of facilitating the necessary changes. The trend is towards smaller training departments and, if these are to have a significant impact on organisational effectiveness, the training that they provide must be such as to add value.

The management of performance

The pre-evaluation will also incorporate stage 4b of the model, as it will be important to examine the context in which performance is expected. The level of performance shown by people in the workplace cannot be predicted from their ability alone, because it is not just a function of knowledge and skills; attitudes are important and so are opportunities and priorities. A better way to predict performance is to look at three aspects:

$$Performance = Ability \times Motivation \times Opportunity$$

The multiplication signs mean that if there is no ability, or no motivation, or no opportunity, there will be a zero level of performance. Each of these three factors needs to be present to some degree.

The decision to use training to improve performance usually implies that ability needs to be increased. However, as we saw above, the level of motivation can also be increased by learning. People who are confident that they can do some task (those who have high self-efficacy) are more likely to attempt it than those whose confidence is low. They are also more likely to persist in trying to do it if it does not go well the first time.

Motivation can be increased in the work context without training the job-holders. Managers can manage performance by setting agreed targets, monitoring progress, assisting when things are not going well, and providing encouragement and praise when things go well. They can also set different priorities and tasks so that the 'opportunity' part of the equation is affected. It could well be that changes in supervisory practice could achieve the desired increase in performance without training the job-holders. If the pre-evaluation establishes that this is the case, then the training investment might be better spent on short 'performance management' workshops for managers.

If the analysis reveals that it is necessary to increase the ability of the job-holders it will often entail a mixture of changing styles of supervision, tasking, performance management and learning to achieve the desired changes in behaviour, and thus effectiveness. This is 'state of the art' training, and evaluation procedures are central to it, because the measurement of performance and the identification of blocks to performance are crucial to success. Managers and supervisors must be involved in these training and development activities because they must set the organisational context to support the learning.

The process which is being described here is one of improving performance by changing the way in which things are done at work. It is, therefore, worthwhile to consider a simple model of organisational change, in order to clarify what is required. Such a model is shown in Figure 5.

Figure 5

TRAINING AS ORGANISATIONAL CHANGE

1 Analyse the existing situation: abilities, blocks, motivation, opportunities → 2 Secure management commitment to changing organisational practices that conflict with development

3 Involve management in programme design and delivery

5 Establish new behaviours in the workplace by some form of performance management ← 4 Carry out the training to improve abilities and confidence

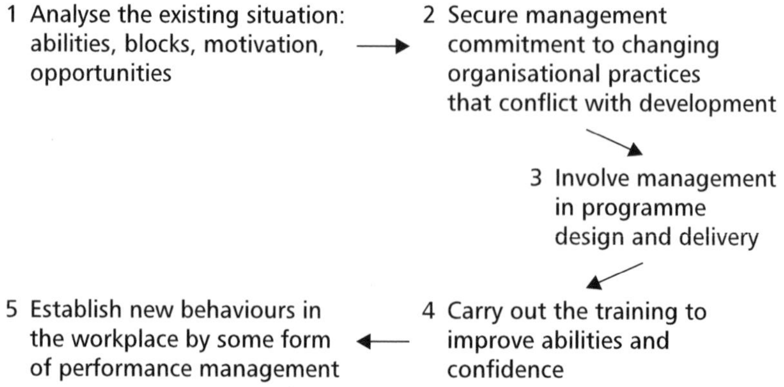

Measurement and evaluation are key aspects of the model in Figure 5. It should also be clear that facilitating the learning is not solely the responsibility of the trainers. The managers or supervisors are also involved to ensure the relevance of what is being learned and continuity of the development of the learning to result in changes in the way that work activities are carried out. They have the important role of assisting transfer of the learning by monitoring and encouraging the new ways of doing the work.

Cost-effectiveness comparisons

Sometimes more than one training approach may be considered. For instance, should we buy someone in to run a particular activity or should we run it with our own people? One of the criteria on which the alternatives should be compared is the cost of providing the training.

It is usually assumed by accountants that the expected outcomes are the same and therefore that one should simply select the cheapest alternative. This may explain the amount of training that is now 'outsourced' to training consultancies. There are, however, added benefits in providing training internally. For instance:

- The training needs analysis might be done more thoroughly by an internal trainer than by a line manager who buys someone in to deal with his problem.
- The internal training department should be better aware of organisational priorities and plans and should, therefore, see more ways of integrating the training with work tasks.
- The mix between what the supervisors will do and what the trainers will do might be easier to agree when the trainer has regular contact with that department on a range of training issues.
- The follow-up evaluation and continuity of learning into the workplace will probably require an internal trainer anyway.

I do not want to be unduly critical of the principle of buying in training. There are many training providers who work on a regular basis with an organisation and who can offer most of the advantages of internal trainers, plus some greater flexibility and experience, at a lower cost. Some, however, are selling standard packages and claim that these can be tailored during the event to suit the delegates' objectives. The perceptive reader of this book will not be surprised to learn that I am suspicious of this. My view is that a careful analysis should be made of the behaviours that need changing in order to improve effectiveness *before* the training is designed.

Cost-benefit analysis

Another aspect of pre-evaluation is that of establishing whether the likely benefits are worth the cost involved in achieving them. Here we are not just asking the question, 'Are there cheaper ways of doing this?' We also need to ask, 'Is it worthwhile doing this at all? What will it cost? What is the likely return?'

Before the learning events are designed, an attempt is made to identify the likely changes in behaviour of those who are to undergo the training. A group of interested parties, usually some of the supervisors/line managers and some of the trainers, discuss what is intended in terms of changes in effectiveness and the behaviours necessary to achieve these. It is often valuable to include the views of other stakeholders (for instance, some of those to be trained and some 'customers' who receive services or products from them) in these discussions.

When the desired changes in behaviour have be identified, each of the stakeholders is asked to list the benefits likely to result from these, seen from his or her perspective. This list of expected benefits can then be compared with the cost of the training and a decision made about whether the investment is worth while. Sometimes the expected benefits can be directly converted to a cash value, but this is not the main purpose of cost-benefit analysis. The intention is to provide a rational basis for making the decision – to train or not train.

Table 15 – taken from reference (1) – is a simple format for summarising the benefit side of the equation. The estimation of the cost side is dealt with in the next section. Cost-benefit analysis can be an involved process, and a full discussion of it is beyond the scope of this book. Readers who are interested in further reading on how to calculate the financial implications of changing organisational procedures are referred to the work of Cascio.[2]

Table 15

COST-BENEFIT ANALYSIS OF A PROPOSED TRAINING EVENT

List of behaviours expected after training	*List of possible benefits to:*
	Trainees
Improved skills	improved job prospects
. . . . .	higher earnings
. . . . .	access to more interesting jobs
. . . . .	improved job satisfaction etc
New skills	
	Supervisors/line managers
. . . . .	increased output
. . . . .	higher value of output
More likely to	more flexible/innovative
. . . . .	likely to stay longer
. . . . .	less likely to be sick/stressed
. . . . .	less likely to be absent
Less likely to	less need to be supervised
. . . . .	increased safety
. . . . .	decrease in accidents etc
. . . . .	
Costs of training	*Customers*
. . . . .	better quality work
. . . . .	less need to return work
. . . . .	more 'on time' deliveries etc

Costing training

It will be necessary to estimate the costs of designing and running the activities. Costing methods and systems will vary, and liaison with the finance department will ensure that the procedure adopted for establishing training costs is compatible with those used in other parts of the organisation. A simple framework for estimating costs that I have found useful is given below.

	Personnel	Facilities	Equipment
Design	1a	1b	1c
Delivery	2a	2b	2c
Evaluation	3a	3b	3c

Design

The cost of design can be spread over the life of the programme (ie shared by the proposed number of programmes) as it may otherwise account for some 50 per cent of the overall costs. As a rough guideline, technical courses will need about five hours' preparation per hour of delivery. Programmed or packaged instruction will be much more expensive, as up to 100 hours of design are needed for one hour of instruction. With computer-based learning the ratio can be as high as 400:1.

Designing the learning event might include such costs as:

1a Costs of preliminary analysis of training needs, development of objectives, course development, lesson planning, programming, audio-visual aids production, consultant advice, contractors.

1b Offices, telephones.

1c Production of workbooks, slides, tapes, tests, programmes, printing and reproduction.

Delivery

The cost of actually running the event might include:

2a Some proportion of the annual salaries of trainers, lecturers, trainees, clerical/admin. staff. Costs of consultants and outside lecturers. Travel costs.

2b   Cost of conference centres or up-keep of classrooms, buildings, offices; accommodation and food; office supplies and expenses.

2c   Equipment for delivering the training – slide projectors, videos, computers, simulators, workbooks, maintenance and repair of aids; expendable training materials or some proportion of the cost relative to life-time; handouts; hire of films, videos etc.

Evaluation   The cost of evaluation is usually low compared to the other two elements. Possible costs include:

3a   Cost of designing questionnaires etc, follow-up interviews, travel, accommodation; analysis and summary of data collected; delivering the evaluation report.

3b   Offices, telephones.

3c   Tests, questionnaires, postage.

To give a complete picture it is also worth considering a general overhead for the expense of maintaining the training department. This may be allocated to individual training programmes on the basis of hours of participant learning, tutor involvement and level of administration required.

Salaries of trainees are often not allocated to training costs on the basis that a certain amount of 'slack' is necessary for effectiveness. For instance, when a foreman is taken off the factory floor for a few hours a week to discuss supervisory methods, it makes very little difference to his 'output' as a foreman. In such a case it seems hardly worth while to include the value of his salary for the hours spent as a cost to training. However, some surveys report that the salary of trainees averages about a third of all training costs. If this is estimated to be a reasonable figure for a programme being planned, then it would seem worthwhile to include these costs. Similarly, I would argue that any 'covering costs' incurred because of trainees' absence from the workplace should be included.

Published studies of cost-benefit usually provide simple statistics of large returns on training investment. For instance, 'return on investment of 8:1', 'investment recovered in only six months' and similar statements. Project work is particularly popular, and the value of the project to the organisation is stated either as a sum or as what it would have cost to have bought in consultants to solve it. These simple statistics usually obscure many of the other things that have happened. The reports on the National Training Awards often describe cascading of priorities, introduction of different working methods and so on – changes to the organisational context as well as increases in ability. It seems to me to be worthwhile trying to capture some of this in the cost–benefit equation, as the process of identifying the need, designing, and carrying out the training may well affect many aspects of the work context.

Matching methods to outcomes

As well as thinking about the mix between training and changes in the organisational context, it is worthwhile considering whether the proposed *methods* are likely to achieve the desired outcomes.

At a basic level this might mean simply that if you want a skilled performance the people need more than just the knowledge of how to do it. They will need to do it a number of times and to practise to improve the level of performance. At a more general level, the evidence is that the approach taken in training should resemble the expected performance.[4]

If you want people to be able to solve particular types of problem – say, when 'trouble-shooting' on a piece of electronic equipment – the best strategy for teaching them to classify and approach problems will be one that teaches them *how* to think – a cognitive approach: how experts would approach the problem, what they would look for, what subgoals they would set, and how they would decide whether they were making progress, because these are the types of learning that would be needed.

If you want supervisors to be able to motivate their subordinates, teaching them theories of motivation will not be sufficient. Theories may be useful to provide frameworks to help the learners make sense of their experience. Knowledge of theory is, however, usually not sufficient to change the way in which people interact with others. A behavioural approach, which encourages them to bring in actual problems, discuss them with other supervisors, role-play them and try out various ways of dealing with the situation, is much more likely to succeed than a theory-based programme.[5,6] The key aspect is that they actually try ways of doing things and then talk about them: they do not just listen to someone telling them how.

One way to think about this is to try to design learning activities that take the learners all the way around the Kolb cycle.[7] A version of this is shown in Figure 6.

Figure 6

THE KOLB CYCLE OF LEARNING

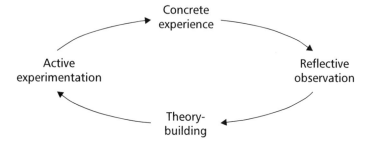

In order to learn effectively, the trainees will need to have some experience. Learning should start from where they are, and needs to be related to their experience if it is to make sense in an organisational context. If they have no experience in the particular area of interest, the training will have to provide it.

As a second stage, they need some framework in which to make sense of the experience. They need to stop and reflect about what the experience means, what aspects of it are important, and so on. Usually they will need to share this reflective stage with others and it often helps if a trainer facilitates this.

The third stage is one of 'theory-building'. This simply means that they change the way in which they think about events like those which they have experienced. In many cases this will entail thinking about ways which might be successful in handling particular situations.

The fourth stage is that of actively trying out some of these ways to see if they will actually be successful. This completes the cycle because it entails further concrete (actual) experience.

It is likely that adults need to go around this cycle a couple of times before they change the way in which they do things. The most successful way to build up self-efficacy is to help the learner to achieve some mastery of the situation by going around a learning cycle like that above.[8] It may be possible for a schoolteacher to convince young children that they can do something by some form of encouragement, but with older children, and certainly with adults, it is usually necessary for them to try it for themselves and thus become convinced that they can do it.

What I am suggesting here is that an important part of the pre-evaluation of a learning activity that is intended to change work behaviours should be to examine whether it will take the trainees all of the way around the cycle. If not, some thought must be given to who will be responsible for 'active experimentation' and consolidation of learning.

Changing attitudes

Changing attitudes is more difficult than changing levels of knowledge or skills. If we are to achieve the higher levels on our continuum (p89) of 'preference for the new methods' and 'incorporation into normal routines', those who are learning will have to change the ways in which they think, and discover advantages in the new ways. This means taking them around the cycle more than once – doing it, thinking about it, trying it in different ways until they are satisfied with the new ways and willing to discard the old.

For example, it has proved to be difficult to teach car drivers to wear seat-belts by merely giving them information. Even when they realise that many injuries can be avoided by wearing a seat- belt, this is not sufficient. It has been found to be necessary to *make* drivers wear them by making it a statutory requirement. One of the effects of this has been that fastening the belt has become incorporated into normal routines for driving. Most people now feel uncomfortable when they have *not* fastened the belt. Their attitudes have changed after they have had to change their behaviour. I am sure that there are many other examples of this in the 'equal opportunities' field, where early approaches were based upon giving information. These have been replaced by statements of what kind of behaviour is expected and the introduction of sanctions for infringing these codes.

In brief

If the intention is to improve performance by changing behaviour, some evaluation should be carried out *before* a learning activity is designed and run in order to decide:

■ whether learning is necessary or whether some form of performance management will achieve the desired changes

■ how the learning will be integrated with other changes

in the organisational context (for instance: goal-setting, priorities, job-design and tasking, structure, climate for innovation)

▌ what level of involvement of supervisors and colleagues will be necessary to support the new ways of carrying out the work.

A further question that should be asked before running training activities is whether the cost is justified by the probable benefits.

▌ When it is thought necessary to carry out the activities, this question may be answered by considering a number of ways of providing the learning opportunities and selecting the one that seems to offer best value for money.

▌ When there is some doubt about the need, a listing of the possible benefits will provide a basis for making the decision.

▌ Where safety or accident rates are concerned, the question may be a rather different one: 'Can we afford *not* to run the training?' This question might also be posed for events that are intended to increase the flexibility of staff or their ability to innovate.

Evaluation before an event might also focus on the proposed methods and ask whether they are likely to be effective in achieving change. Knowledge and theory may be necessary but, if behavioural change is expected, some practice of the type of behaviour expected will be required. A sound, general principle of training design is that methods should be matched to outcomes. Some of the expected outcomes are actually forms of organisational change and, where this is the case, aspects of the organisational context will need to be considered. For instance, it may be necessary to change the reward system (by encouragement and sanctions) as well as attitudes and levels of knowledge.

This pre-activity evaluation of the likelihood that a proposed training activity will result in the increased performance desired is a key aspect of evaluation as 'control'. In my experience it is often carried out without any degree of sophistication. This is usually because the links between those responsible for training and line managers are not close enough to make it possible.

> What is happening in your organisation? Have you put procedures in place to ensure that most of the investment in training will result in improved performance?

References

1   BRAMLEY P. and B. KITSON 'Evaluating training against business criteria.' *Journal of European Industrial Training*. **18**, 1, (1994) 10–14

2   CASCIO W. F. *Costing Human Resources: The financial impact of behaviour in organisations*. (3rd Edn) Boston, PWS-Kent. (1991)

3   WEINSTEIN L.M. and E.S. KASL 'How the training dollar is spent'. *Training and Development Journal*. (October 1982)

4   GOLDSTEIN I.L. and ASSOCIATES *Training and Development in Organisations*. San Francisco, Jossey-Bass. (1989) (Particularly Chapter 7 by Latham, Chapter 5 by Howell and Cooke, and Chapter 13 by Campbell)

5   GOLDSTEIN A.P. and M. SORCHER *Changing Supervisor Behavior*. New York, Pergammon Press. (1974)

6   LATHAM G.P. and L.M. SAARI 'The application of social learning theory to training supervisors through behavioural modeling.' *Journal of Applied Psychology*. **64** (1979) 239–246.

7   KOLB D.A. *Experiential Learning*, Englewood Cliffs, NJ, Prentice-Hall. (1984)

8   BANDURA A. *Social Foundations of Thought and Action*. Englewood Cliffs, NJ, Prentice-Hall. (1986)

8

Evaluation during the Event

Stage 6 of our model of training is an acknowledgement that learning activities are required to facilitate changes in behaviour and effectiveness. If these activities are to be carried out efficiently and effectively, evaluation should be used during the learning process to ensure that it meets the objectives set for it by the various interested parties. Evaluation can also be used to 'benchmark' the design and delivery of the activities against best practice.

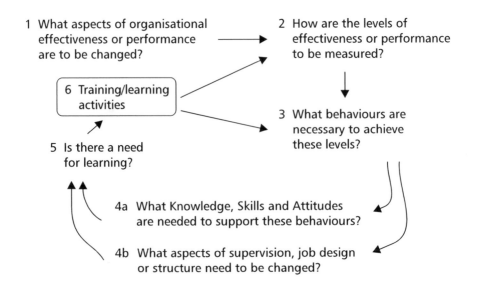

1 What aspects of organisational effectiveness or performance are to be changed?

2 How are the levels of effectiveness or performance to be measured?

6 Training/learning activities

3 What behaviours are necessary to achieve these levels?

5 Is there a need for learning?

4a What Knowledge, Skills and Attitudes are needed to support these behaviours?

4b What aspects of supervision, job design or structure need to be changed?

Establishing the objectives

The clarification of the objectives, the reasons for learning and the expectations of the three main interested parties (usually the trainees, their managers and the organisation) are important as a basis for later evaluation. The processes involved in this are, of course, also necessary for the design of the activities and their integration into organisational priorities. The objectives that are of most value are those that are quite specific about what kinds of behaviour change is expected, ie what employees will be able to do that they could not do before, what they will do more, and what they will do less. Such objectives set targets for the learning and are thus motivating for the learners, provided they accept some 'ownership' of the targets.[1]

One aspect of evaluating is therefore to establish that the trainees have objectives, that these are in line with those of other interested parties and that the trainees are, to some extent, committed to achieving them. A well-organised training system will usually ensure that this is done *before* the programme of learning begins. The line manager, together with a trainer, will establish exactly what is the training need. The trainee will be involved in this, at least to the extent of discussing with the line manager what the objectives are and what changes are expected. When the programme is a long one, it may also be worthwhile for the trainer/tutor to talk at some length with the trainee about aims and objectives, possible content and style of delivery.

Where this does not happen, the early part of the programme itself will need to be used to establish what the objectives are and to create some desire to learn what is necessary to achieve them. There are many ways in which this might be done.

With off-the-job programmes of more than two days it may be possible to interview each of the participants in the evenings and talk these things over in a fairly informal way. Questions that might be useful for this are:

- How did you hear about the programme?
- Why did you want to come on it?
- What are you hoping to get out of it?
- How will this help you in your work?
- How is it going so far?
- Are the methods being used helping you to learn?
- Is there anything we should be doing differently?

One purpose of this is to try to assess how close the programme is to what the trainees expected (that is, how good the pre-course information and briefing were). Another is to try to discover variations in the objectives of the participants, which might entail some re-design of the remaining parts of the programme. A third is to try to discover if the methods, pace and level of difficulty are suitable for the participants.

It is also possible to distribute copies of the aims and objectives that were set for the trainers who designed the programme, and discuss these with the participants. This tends to be a rather one-way process: the trainers telling the trainees what is in store. It is sometimes possible to involve the participants by asking them to describe what they will do differently when they go back, if they can achieve these objectives. The value in this is that it might encourage the trainees to take more 'ownership' of the objectives and thus the learning.

Some tutors ask the participants to write their objectives on flipchart paper and decorate the walls with these. This process does create a sense of 'ownership' and allows individual trainees to discover possible objectives other than those which they have recorded. It is also possible to review progress against these objectives at the end of the workshop. A possible danger in using this process is that the objectives set by the participants may have little to do with effectiveness in the workplace. For instance, I have often seen a display of objectives for an interpersonal skills workshop which looked to me like requests for personal therapy. I would prefer a process that provided a stronger link with changed behaviour and effectiveness in the workplace.

Discussion of progress

An extension of establishing the objectives to motivate the participants to learn is to hold reviews of progress. Reviewing progress and giving feedback has a motivational aspect in that it clarifies, for the learner, the gap between present and desired performance. It is usually necessary for the trainee to be aware of these gaps and be willing to do something about them if learning is to occur. It also has the function of establishing, for the tutors, what learning has taken place and what is still needed. This information may be necessary for the (re-)design of the later stages in the programme.

One way of doing this is to have regular learning reviews, at which the participants write down what they have found to be particularly interesting or useful during the session. Ask them to take a sheet of paper, perhaps of a different colour, and then to write down the two or three things that they have found particularly interesting. Also ask them to write down the two or three things that they think will be most useful to them when they return to the workplace. Ask them to make a note of how they intend to use these and what they think will result from this use. The subsequent discussion can be as a group, where everyone selects something to read out, or one-to-one with tutors. The discussion should give a good feel for what is going well and what learning they are likely to take away. It can also be used to facilitate some 'reflection' on the learning process.

The frequency of these reviews is a matter of judgement. In a programme of some weeks' duration, a review at the end of each week would seem to be appropriate. I have found that on a four-day workshop each evening is a good frequency. Perhaps the most valuable purpose of these reviews is to focus on the usefulness of the learning during the programme. This is again an attempt to set benchmarks against good practice. The process can also give a basis for later evaluation of any changes. Those aspects that participants have found interesting and potentially useful can be grouped into clusters towards the end of the programme to form an action plan. This takes them further around the learning cycle to 'active experimentation'. The action plan can be used as a basis for establishing what they intend to do in the six months after the programme, and it can later be used to assess what they have actually achieved.

Developing and using action plans

There is little doubt that a good deal of adult behaviour is motivated by setting goals. People have plans for what they want to do, how far they want to be promoted, how they are going to impress senior people to achieve this, where they would like to be working in five years' time, and so on. There is also little doubt that setting these goals affects performance, both in terms of direction and effort.[1] The greatest value of action-planning is that it taps into these sources of motivation and can thus provide a bridge for transferring learning to the work situation.

The action plans that experienced people produce are different from those made by novices. They are more specific and the subgoals are more clearly and logically linked to the ultimate goals. One method of evaluating during a learning activity is to examine the quality of the action plans which the participants are producing. The plans should be lists of statements ranked in some way. This might be by order of priority, chronological order or in some other logical sequence. Against each statement there should be a time-frame for action. The links between the statements should be established and, where there is likely to be some difficulty in making one of these links or achieving one of the actions, a 'force-field analysis' is carried out. This simply means thinking and then writing down:

The action: _____

Those things (or people) likely to hinder achievement of the action:	Those things (or people) likely to help achieve this action:
a	*a*
b	*b*
c	*c*
d	*d*

The action plan is an excellent basis for follow-up of the programme. A copy might be lodged with the tutors and used for this purpose. (It should, of course, be thoroughly discussed with the line manager on return, and this would probably be the first action listed on it.) The follow-up, some six months later, would ask such questions as:

▌ How much of your action plan have you been able to implement?

▌ Which actions are still likely but now need a longer time- frame?

▌ Which actions have been shelved, and why?

▌ What positive organisational benefits have come from your actions?

Learning logs and learning contracts can provide action plans during the training activities and provide links between them. They can be used to check on progress and provide the basis for a follow-up interview. In the work on the use of subordinate feedback for changing the styles used by middle managers mentioned earlier (p43), a learning contract was drawn up by each of the managers. They were given the feedback from their subordinates and then asked if there was anything positive that they could take from it. They were then asked to make out an action plan that listed what they intended to do, how they were going to do it, and how they were going to check on progress. Each signed his or her plan as a 'learning contract' (the format is shown in Table 16) with the consultant and it was made the basis of a six-month review of progress. It was also used as a basis for discussion, and further planning, after the one year follow-up of subordinates' opinions on how the style had changed.[2]

Table 16

A LEARNING CONTRACT

Objectives set	Strategy for achieving the objectives	Criteria and means of evaluating progress
Objective 1	How you intend to do it	How you intend to measure achievement
Objective 2	"	"
Objective 3	"	"
etc		
etc		
Date:	Signed:	Signed:

Reactions at the end of an activity

The most popular form of evaluation is the issue of a questionnaire during, or at the end of, the programme. The purpose is said to be that it provides feedback for the tutors so that they can improve future courses. Sometimes the ratings are also used by the training manager to monitor the quality of the programme.

If the intention is to provide feedback to improve the quality of the programme, what information is required? In the Introduction there is a list (page 6) at which you might glance to refresh your memory. The aspect that concerns us here is, 'Some detail about the effectiveness of each learning situation.' If this is to be collected, a format such as that in Table 17 would help. Here all of the topics covered are listed, and a series of questions asked about each.

Table 17

END-OF-COURSE QUESTIONNAIRE

In columns 'b' and 'c' select a number that represents your opinion using the following scales:

Almost all of the information was new	1 2 3 4 5	Told me little I didn't already know
Presentation needs no improvement	1 2 3 4 5	Presentation needs much improvement

a Topic	*b* New information	*c* Presentation	*d* Time			*e* This was difficult
			More	Less	Right	
Topic 1	1 2 3 4 5	1 2 3 4 5				
Topic 2	1 2 3 4 5	1 2 3 4 5				
Topic 3	1 2 3 4 5	1 2 3 4 5				
etc						

The participants should be encouraged to make open-ended comments on the back of the form. Where someone has admitted 'difficulty' this should be followed up to discover the problem.

Specific open-ended questions can be included in the questionnaire to provide information thought to be useful. Common questions are:

■ What are the three best things about this course?
■ What are the three worst things about this course?
■ What three changes should be made to the course?
■ What aspects of the process helped you to learn?
■ What aspects hindered your learning?

If it is to provide really useful information, the question-naire should be given out at the beginning of the programme and time should be allowed so that it can be completed stage by stage. On programmes that last longer than a week, collecting and reviewing the forms at the end of each week might help with the detailed planning of the following week's work.

It should be clear from this that considerable detail is necessary to provide the feedback required to review the effectiveness of each learning situation. This should be worthwhile for the first two runs of a programme, when many amendments may need to be made to the order of events and to specific activities. After the first two or so runs most of the benefit of such feedback will have been realised. When this is the case, a more economical evaluative procedure is to focus on new topics only. Questions such as those in Table 18 could be asked about each of these new topics.

Table 18

QUESTIONS ABOUT A TOPIC

▌ What is your overall reaction to the
   session on . . . . ?   Very good/Good/Fair/Poor

▌ Will you be able to use the material
   (or skill) in your job?   Frequently/Sometimes/Rarely/Unlikely

▌ What did you think of the
   presentation of the session?   Very good/Good/Fair/Poor

▌ How do you think the session could
   be improved?

Most organisations carry out evaluation at the 'reaction' level.[3,4] Trainers obviously believe that it is important to discover how participants feel about the programme which they have attended. Perhaps they are making an assumption that favourable reactions imply useful learning, or will predict changes in behaviour; there is not much evidence to support this. The published studies in which attempts have been made to correlate levels of reaction with the amount of learning or changes in work behaviour or levels of effectiveness have shown very poor correlations.[5] In general, *good* reactions do not predict learning or behaviour change or increased effectiveness any better than poor reactions. This is probably because the information being gathered is not suitable for that purpose. Inspection of a typical set of forms usually reveals that what is being assessed is whether the training was enjoyable and interesting rather than useful; whether the accommodation was comfortable; whether the tutors were liked. This is training as a branch of entertainment: these factors may have nothing to do with learning that might support increased effectiveness.

If the completion of these forms is to be more than an end-of-course ritual it is important to make sure that the information can provide useful feedback. General questions like:

How would you rate the course overall?   POOR 1 2 3 4 5 EXCELLENT

How would you rate the tutors?   POOR 1 2 3 4 5 EXCELLENT

do not provide information that is specific enough for this purpose.

If the intention is to provide feedback on specific tutors, some of the questions listed in Table 7 (p 81) might be useful. I feel certain that rating all of the tutors, or even one of them, on a five-point scale is a waste of time.

Similarly, I am very dubious about attempting to discover if the objectives of the programme have been achieved by asking:

Did the course meet your objectives?   NOT AT ALL 1 2 3 4 5 TOTALLY

If, as was suggested earlier, the objectives of the various interested parties have been made specific, then more precise ways will be available of assessing whether they have been achieved. Most of these evaluations will be made in the workplace and not at the end of training.

I do not want to give the impression that I am against the principle of using questionnaires to collect information about courses. The practice, however, often seems to be a meaningless ritual because not enough thought has been given to the reasons for collecting the information and, therefore, to the type of information that would be useful.

Evaluating the running of a programme

When a programme has been running for some time it may be possible to improve its effectiveness by examining the its whole process. It is more likely that this would be done by a training manager than by the trainers themselves, but a check-list of questions to ask might help to focus on good practice. The following list of questions was developed to focus on key areas when carrying out inspections of training organisations.[6]

Target population

∎ Are the 'right' people coming on to the programme?

∎ Are they coming at the right time?

∎ Are they being briefed properly before they come?

∎ What proportion are on the programme for such reasons as: a rest; her turn for training; someone else dropped out?

Objectives

∎ What changes are expected to result from this programme in terms of:

☐ individual performance levels?

☐ organisational effectiveness?

∎ Are the objectives clear and unambiguous?

∎ Do the tutors know the trainees' individual learning

objectives? How are they taking these into account?

Course structure

- On what learning principles is the programme structured?
- Is there a satisfactory balance between practice, reflection and theoretical input?
- Is the programme the right length?
- Does the balance of the course reflect the different degrees of importance attached to the objectives?

Methods and media

- On what basis have the methods been chosen?
- Are behavioural methods being used where behavioural change is expected?
- Are mental maps being built up where problem-solving is expected?
- Are the characteristics of the learners being considered?
- Do the methods and media provide variety and encourage learning?
- What is the quality and readability of handouts, computer-based training material and training aids?

Evaluative feedback

- How is progress being assessed during the programme?
- Is each assessment method reliable and timely?
- How is feedback given to the trainees?
- How is feedback used by the tutors? Is there enough flexibility to allow for its use?

In brief

Evaluation during a learning activity can be a useful source of information with which to improve the quality of the event.

One aspect which is worth considering is the clarification of the objectives so that there is a shared understanding of what the learners and the tutors are trying to achieve. Some method of relating the objectives to organisational goals should also be established. Methods for achieving this link are described in Chapter 2 and also in reference (7).

Reviewing the progress of the learning during the event is an extension of the process of establishing shared objectives. A focus on utility of the learning and action-planning for application of it in the workplace will reinforce the link between objectives of the event and organisational requirements.

Information gathered by questionnaire at the end of a learning event is too late to be useful in improving the quality of the activities that have already been run. If the information is to be used to improve the quality of future events very careful selection of questions is necessary. It will also be necessary to justify the belief that the next set of participants will require the same learning experience in order to achieve their objectives.

General questions and overall ratings are of little value for the purpose of 'feedback' on the quality of the course. These ratings are subject to many sources of bias and do not predict either the amount of learning or the likelihood of future behavioural change. Where the interest is in the performance of the tutors, a better source of information is a check-list of behaviour such as that in Table 7. Where the interest is in the programme as a whole, the questions listed in Table 18 will provide relevant data.

References

1   LOCKE E.A. and G.P. LATHAM *A Theory of Goal-setting and Task Performance*. Englewood Cliffs NJ, Prentice-Hall. (1990)

2   BRAMLEY P. 'Using Subordinate Appraisals as Feedback.' Paper given to the 23rd International Congress of Applied Psychology, Madrid. Copies available from the Department of Organizational Psychology, Birkbeck College, University of London. (1994)

3   RALPHS L.T. and E. STEPHAN 'HRD in the Fortune 500'. *Training and Development Journal*. **40**, (1986) 69–76

4   *Training in Britain: A Study of Funding, Activity and Attitudes*. London, HMSO. (1989)

5   ALLIGER G.M. and E.A. JANAK 'Kirkpatrick's levels of training criteria: thirty years later'. *Personnel Psychology*. **42**, (1989) 331–342

6   BRAMLEY P. and H. HULLAH 'Auditing training.' *Journal of European Industrial Training*. **11**, 6, (1987) 5–10

7   BOYDELL T. and L. LEARY *Identifying Training Needs*. London, IPD. (1996)

9

Approaches to Evaluation

We have now come full circle by discussing how to establish evaluative criteria in each of the stages of the training model. Techniques have been described which should make it possible to evaluate changes in effectiveness and behaviour and also the quality and quantity of learning. In this final chapter the focus is on the underlying philosophy of evaluation rather than the techniques. The questions addressed are:

▌ What sort of process is evaluation?

▌ What sort of process should it be?

Formulating answers to these questions will identify the kind of information that needs to be collected and the methods by which it should be gathered.

Evaluation, as a professional area of expertise, has developed from attempts to improve the quality of education. The main approach advocated has been influenced by historical and economic factors, and three distinct phases can be identified. Early attempts at evaluation emphasised measurement and testing, assessing whether pupils had learned what might be expected of children of their age. A later development was the introduction of objectives to control the curriculum. Evaluation of a programme could then be made by assessing the extent to which these objectives had been achieved. More recent approaches have acknowledged that views of the strengths and weaknesses of particular programmes will differ. Evaluation following this sort of approach is a process of collecting the views of a sample of interested parties and summarising them. The evaluation report will show what consensus exists and identify where there are significant differences in the opinions of the interested parties.

Evaluation as testing

Testing people's knowledge and skills is still an important part of learning within the world of work. Assessment of present levels and setting goals for the achievement of higher levels is an important source of motivation to learn. Post-learning examinations and tests are also used to ensure that people reach a certain set standard, and hence that applicants are qualified in aspects of technical education needed for their work. Success in tests of knowledge and skills is also a criterion for membership of many professional bodies. The standards against which candidates will be judged are set by committees of experienced members, and the method of assessment will usually also be agreed within this forum. Evaluation is a process of deciding what the standards are, how to test whether candidates have reached them and making an assessment of each individual candidate. Some of the problems involved in doing this have been discussed in Chapters 4 and 5, and some of the methods that can be used have been described.

Tests may also be used for purposes of comparison. Results may be used to compare the ability of individuals and thus to predict effectiveness. There are some technical problems involved in this. The most difficult is probably that of establishing that the test situation is sufficiently reliable to allow predictions to be made. The Appendix includes a discussion of how to establish test reliability. Tests which are diagnostic in nature (such as 'trainability tests' or 'assessment centre' tasks), may also be used to identify areas of weakness which need correcting by some developmental process.

Evaluation by testing knowledge and skills has a place within an organisational context, but it will rarely be sufficient on its own. Employees will use knowledge and skills to perform tasks in the workplace, and their ability to apply them to work tasks is also important. This suggests setting up the testing situation to reflect, as accurately as is possible, the work situation, which brings us to a second approach to evaluation.

Evaluation as meeting objectives

After the First World War a good deal of experimentation took place in educational establishments. Education was becoming much more widely available and it was recognised that the greater range of abilities among pupils might require different approaches. Evaluation was necessary to compare the value of new and progressive school curricula with more conventional ones. To try to produce some common ground for comparison purposes it was suggested that the curricula needed to be organised by the use of objectives. Objectives were seen as being crucial because they were the basis for planning, for guiding the instruction, and for the preparation of test and assessment procedures. The process of evaluation that was proposed[1] had a number of phases:

1. Collect, from as wide a consultation as possible, a pool of objectives that might be related to the curriculum.

2. Screen the objectives carefully to select a subset that covers the desirable changes.

3. Express these objectives in terms of the student behaviours that are expected.

4. Develop instruments for testing each objective. These must meet acceptable standards of objectivity, reliability and validity.

5. Apply the instruments before and after the learning experiences.
6. Examine the results to discover strengths and any weaknesses in the curriculum.
7. Develop hypotheses about reasons for weaknesses and attempt to rectify these.
8. Modify the curriculum and recycle the process.

This sounds like a very logical and sensible way of designing an educational system and I have quoted it in full because it also has great relevance to training in organisations. Would that we all had the time and the ability to do this for each of our training programmes!

The educational establishment, at least in the UK, did very little to develop this work into a rationale for school curricula. After the Second World War further developmental work on the structure of knowledge[2] was also largely ignored by the educational establishment. Indeed, it is only now in the 1990s that the UK Government has started to force this way of thinking onto an unwilling educational establishment through the introduction of the core curriculum.

The use of objectives did, however, strike a chord with those interested in training within organisations. Work on programmed instruction[3] led to the development of a behavioural-objectives approach to technical education and training. These objectives contain three statements:

▌ A description of the performance that is to be demonstrated. This should be an observable behaviour which demonstrates that the candidate can do something; mere understanding is not enough.
▌ The conditions under which this performance is to be tested. These conditions should closely resemble those when performing the task in the workplace.
▌ The standards that are considered to be acceptable. These should be related to adequate job performance levels.

The trainees are offered these detailed objectives as goals, and evaluation is a matter of assessing how many of them have been attained by individuals and groups. The process has proved to be very successful in improving the effectiveness and efficiency of training. There are three main reasons for this:

■ The objectives are simulations of key job tasks. When they are achieved they ensure task mastery, and thus transfer of training.

■ The objectives direct the attention of the trainees and allow them to self-set the goals, thus building motivation into the learning situation.

■ Because the objectives are agreed by a committee rather than by a trainer, and on the basis of careful job analysis rather than out-of-date experience, the resulting training has a very sharp focus on 'need-to-know'. It is therefore much more efficient and usually more effective than 'learn as much as you can'.

There are, however, a number of problems with this approach to controlling and evaluating training. The objectives are often difficult to write, and sometimes they represent what can be easily tested rather than what should be learned. The trainers, particularly those who enjoy demonstrating their expertise, may feel that many of the key decisions about how to design and run courses have been removed from them. The process clearly identifies where the training is not going well, and this increased level of accountability is difficult for some trainers to accept. (My own view is that this is why this approach has never been accepted within education.)

The approach is still used very successfully in the armed forces, where it was originally developed, and in some other large organisations where there is a good deal of technical operative training. It has never really been accepted within management training and development, where how people carry out tasks is regarded as being less important than how they discharge their responsibilities.

Something very like the behavioural objectives approach is now being introduced into many organisations, again under pressure from the UK Government, through the use of National Vocational Qualifications (NVQs). These require the demonstration of abilities in a work-related context, rather than teaching and examining technical skills within a classroom. The way in which the skills are described and the format for testing has clearly been influenced by the work on behavioural objectives.

Part of the reason why this approach has not been more widely accepted is that objectives are being set as tests of job tasks. Many argue that evaluation should not be just about behaviour: that there are other aspects which are of interest. This has led to a number of attempts to specify objectives at a number of levels. The first important contribution, and still the most influential,[4] proposed that objectives should be set for four levels:

1. the *reactions* of the trainees to the programme: what they thought of it

2. measuring the amount of *learning* of principles, facts, skills and attitudes

3. changes in *behaviour* in the job

4. *results*: changes in criteria of organisational effectiveness.

It was pointed out in Chapter 8 that most organisations carry out evaluations at the reactions level; some measure learning in technical training; but few attempt the higher levels.[5,6] I hope that the readers of this book will feel more confident in doing this, as setting objectives at these levels was the subject of Chapters 2 and 3. It is not easy to set objectives at these levels, but it is possible, and it is becoming more and more necessary to do so. The logic of this objectives-based approach is that goals should be set at each level before the learning activities are designed. These objectives form the basis for later evaluation which should establish the extent to which they have been achieved.

The setting of learning objectives is also to be recommended for on-the-job development and activities other than off-the-job courses. The developing employee and the supervisor (perhaps assisted by a member of the training department) analyse the possibilities of learning within the tasks to be done over (say) the next six months. A learning contract is then drawn up which specifies some four to six objectives to be achieved during the period. A simple format for such a contract was shown in Table 16.

Most trainers, when advising others on how to evaluate training, use some form of setting objectives, usually at the four levels listed above. This is not surprising: deciding what the training is intended to achieve, pre-setting objectives to specify what effects should be seen, and then evaluating whether they have been achieved is a sound way to ensure effective training. In practice, however, it is often difficult to produce clear links between training objectives and organisational goals. Given the trend of looking for organisational returns from training investment, it is a serious problem.

An important aspect of this problem is the extent to which the objectives of a programme are shared. If there is a high degree of consensus about what the programme should achieve, then objectives-based evaluation should be possible. Experience of using impact analysis (p13) suggests that there is often a wide range of views about a programme. For instance, in a study carried out by one of my students, representatives from production, marketing and finance had very different views about an MSc programme in engineering which was being sponsored by a manufacturing organisation. Another example, from the public sector, was the widely different views expressed about the Children's Act and its implications, by residential social workers, social sorkers involved in fostering, and representatives of the finance function.

What is your view? In your experience, is an organisation *one* group of people with shared goals and common purpose? An alternative view, which recognises the political aspect of organisations, is that organisations are made up of several groups of people, each with different goals. If this is the case, an approach to evaluation that recognises it might be more appropriate than one that assumes shared objectives.

Responsive evaluation

Responsive evaluation[7] has been developed over the last 20 years to cope with the situation where the evaluator is less concerned with the stated objectives of the programme than with how it is seen by various interested parties – the 'stakeholders'. These stakeholders will usually fall into three broad classes:

■ agents who run or use the programme that is to be evaluated

■ beneficiaries who profit in some way from the use of the programme

■ victims who suffer in some way because of the programme.[8]

For a training programme these are likely to be: the staff organising the programme, those delivering it, and a sample of those who will be affected by it (participants, their supervisors and more senior line managers).

The evaluator will talk to these stakeholders and ask them what they have to say about the programme that is positive (their claims), and what concerns they have about it. It helps in this if the evaluator has first of all observed a run of the programme and has some feel for what it is trying to do and how it is trying to do it. Different stakeholders will often have different claims and concerns and the function of the evaluator is to identify these and to produce a report which shows:

- what consensus there is about the programme
- what issues there are about which people disagree.

This report is circulated to representatives of the main stakeholder groups who then become aware of the claims and concerns of others. The issues which have been identified will probably need further investigation to discover if they are due to lack of information or some deeper cause.

The circulation of this interim report will affect the way in which the stakeholders think about the programme. It is thus an intervention in its own right, and the evaluator has become part of the process rather than an observer of it. There usually is a second phase of planning further evaluation to satisfy the various issues and concerns. The direction of the evaluation is thus not fixed at the outset, but re-adjusted as data become available.

My experience of using this kind of evaluative process is that line managers welcome being involved and value the opportunity to express their views. They are often impressed that trainers should talk to them in this way and they usually become more sympathetic to training initiatives generally, whether or not they value the particular programme under discussion.

The underlying philosophy of responsive evaluation is very different from that of following up objectives. It does not set out to discover the 'truth' of whatever has been achieved by the training programme. Rather, it sets out to 'construct' the truth as seen from a number of different perspectives. It is not part of the strict scientific approach where causes are sought. It is an example of action research in which the interested parties collect the data, make some sense of it and then decide what to do next.

The strength of responsive evaluation is that it is a collaboration between the evaluator and the key stakeholders, and it takes into account different perspectives. Where organisations are trying to use training programmes as a part of a change process, this will be necessary in order to tailor the intervention to the needs of the various subgroups. Change implies influencing people and a powerful method of achieving this is to consult and involve them. If, as some would argue, the nature of organisational change is essentially political, an evaluative approach which recognises this political dimension should be more appropriate than one which does not.

In brief

Evaluation, if it is to be more than merely the expression of a few opinions, involves gathering information with which to answer particular questions. This information needs to be reliable, in the sense of being representative and relevant to the purpose. In Chapter 1 it was suggested that purposes for evaluation could be grouped under three main headings – feedback, control and intervention.

Feedback

Testing knowledge and skills before and after a training event will provide information on the efficiency of the event in producing changes. Gains can be measured in specific areas and thus average gains for the whole group or for specific subgroups can be calculated. The strength of evaluation as testing is that it can be used to provide feedback on the quality of training events.

Evaluation by setting goals and measuring the extent of their achievement can also provide useful feedback. In this case, much of the evidence is about application of the learning in the workplace, how relevant it is and how effective.

Control

If the evaluative question is a one of control (for example, whether the programme results in increased effectiveness, or whether the programme should be run at all), tests of knowledge and skills will not be able to provide the relevant information.

Some of the control questions can be answered by an evaluation of the extent to which objectives have been achieved. If this sort of information is to be generated by an objectives-based evaluation, three conditions need to be met:

■ The objectives should be expressed in terms of behaviour to be demonstrated in the workplace.

■ Links between these behaviours and effectiveness need to be made by demonstrating the relationship between the objectives for training and performance or meeting goals within a part of the organisation.

■ There needs to be a high level of consensus between interested parties on the objectives to be achieved.

A wider set of control questions can be answered by using a responsive approach. Whether key purposes are being met can be discussed with a wide range of stakeholders, and thus a list of benefits established. This information can be related to the cost of the programme and provide a basis for some 'control' decisions.

Intervention   All three approaches offer opportunities to use evaluation as an intervention into organisational processes. The testing approach offers opportunities to improve the selection of trainees as it can clarify the specification of the target population in terms of levels of knowledge and skills. Discussion of results might also increase the communication between training and the line, but there may be problems with disclosing test results.

Setting and evaluating the achievement of objectives should involve supervisors and line managers. This involvement can be a powerful way of improving the briefing before the event and extending the learning after the programme because of supervisor interest etc.

The responsive approach to evaluation is a deliberate attempt to intervene. The perceptions that stakeholders have about the programme and their level of involvement with it will change as a result of the process of collecting information.

References

1   TYLER R.W. *Basic Principles of Curriculum and Instruction Design*. Chicago, University of Chicago Press. (1950)

2   BLOOM B.S. *Taxonomy of Educational Objectives: Cognitive Domain*. London, Longmans. (1956)

3   MAGER R.F. *Preparing Objectives for Programmed Instruction*. San Francisco, Fearon. (1962)

4   KIRKPATRICK D.L. 'Techniques for evaluating training programmes'. *Journal of the American Society of Training Directors*. **13**, (1959) 3–9 and 21–26; **14**, 13–18 and 28–32

5   RALPHS L.T. and E. STEPHAN 'HRD in the Fortune 500'. *Training and Development Journal*. **40**, (1986) 69–76

6   *Training in Britain: A study of funding, activity and attitudes*. London, HMSO. (1989)

7   STAKE R.E. (Ed) *Evaluating the Arts in Education: A responsive approach*. Columbus, Ohio, Merrill. (1975)

8   GUBA E.G. and Y.S. LINCOLN *Fourth Generation Evaluation*. Beverly Hills, CA, Sage. (1989)

A

Appendix:
Reliability of Testing

Reliability of testing is an important issue but, within the field of training, one that is largely neglected. Many of the short tests which are used to assess learning are not reliable measures. Unreliable measures will produce estimates of knowledge or skills that may look precise but will be misleading. For instance, imagine yourself in the situation of trying, by use of tests, to grade 100 young job applicants into the following proportions:

A	B	C	D	E
10%	20%	40%	20%	10%

Your intention is to offer jobs to the top 30% and put the next 40% onto a waiting-list.

If you did the grading on the basis of height, and you measured the height of each one carefully, you could expect to allocate the tallest 10 to grade A, the next 20 to grade B and so on. One or two might be in the wrong grade because of some 'human error' of measurement. This would imply some unreliability in the testing situation – 'to err is human' – but there should be very little of it. (You would, of course, find yourself in some difficulty about proving the suitability of the test for the purpose, ie its *validity*. It seems certain that someone would ask you to prove this, as the test would discriminate against female candidates.)

Height was chosen as an example of a measure that is reliable. It is, however, rarely an important criterion in job selection. But suppose that you work in the financial sector and that the jobs entail a good deal of numerical work. You set the applicants a test of one hundred short questions on arithmetic. How much unreliability would you expect? How many candidates do you think would be allocated to the wrong grades because of unreliability of the testing situation? The answer might surprise you, as it would probably be about 20 per cent of them. Why should this be?

■ You are sampling their knowledge by using only a hundred questions to estimate their total knowledge. This is a source of unreliability because the actual questions asked will suit some of them better than others.

■ People tend to perform better on some days than others. Are you measuring the best that they can do or something much lower than that because they are not well, or overtired?

■ Some people perform better early in the morning and others do not really wake up until later in the day.

■ Some people are really motivated by test situations and rise to the challenge; others find that test situations make them anxious and they underperform.

■ Some errors will be made in the scoring.

This inevitable unreliability in the testing situation is the main reason why selection at eleven-plus for grammar school education became indefensible. It was (and is) impossible to pick out the top 20 per cent and not get some youngsters on the wrong side of the decision line. If the tests are used to stream them into three or four classes in the same school the mistakes are not so serious, as they can be rectified during the year by careful monitoring of performance. If the test results are used to allocate the young people to different schools then it is very difficult to correct the mistaken decisions.

It must surely be important to establish that measures are reliable if important decisions are to be made on the basis of test results. Tests that have low reliability are providing incorrect information, and this is useless for the purpose of making good decisions.

Estimating test reliability

Reliability can be estimated and expressed as a figure which runs from zero (no reliability) to 1 (completely reliable). In the example of trying to allocate 100 people to five grades, different levels of reliability will give the following proportions of people who will be wrongly graded:

Reliability	=	1.0	Wrongly graded	=	0%
	=	0.9		=	23%
	=	0.8		=	33%
	=	0.7		=	40%
	=	0.5		=	50%

At what level would you say that the test results should be ignored as a source of data for decision-making? I would argue that if the reliability falls below 0.8, the results are, to say the least, misleading.

If a test is reliable it will give consistent results; those who are good will obtain good scores each time they attempt it, and those who are poor will obtain poor marks. The classic way to estimate test reliability is to use the test twice on the same group of candidates. A reliable test will give much the same rank order on each occasion; the same people will be at or near the top and the candidates who were at or near the bottom on the first test will also be there on the re-test. A good example of a reliable test situation is the one above of measuring height. Measuring the same person a number of times would give very similar results. Where tests are samples of something they will be less reliable, because there is always a problem of estimating the whole from a sample.

Test/retest reliability

Using our example of 100 questions in arithmetic, let us assume that the candidates were tested twice and the results of 20 of them were:

Candidate	A	B	C	D	E	F	G	H	J	K	L	M	N	O	P	Q	R	S	T	U
Test	91	83	76	68	66	64	62	60	59	58	56	56	55	53	52	51	50	49	46	43
Retest	93	86	75	66	60	63	58	68	49	50	58	62	58	40	49	50	41	55	50	46

Plotting the two sets of scores on a scattergram allows us to estimate reliability by eye, and a simple calculation will help us to decide whether the reliability is higher than 0.8, and therefore acceptable, or less than this figure.

First the plots: A has two scores in the 90s and goes into the top right-hand cell. Similarly B with two 80s and C with two 70s. The candidate R has 50 on the test and 41 on the retest ie cell 50+/40+. The full set of plots is shown in Figure A1.

Figure A1

A SCATTERGRAM

Test Score

	40−	40+	45+	50+	55+	60+	65+	70+	80+	90+
90+										A
80+									B	
70+								C		
65+						E	D			
60+					G	F	H			
55+			J	K	N L	M				
50+		R O	P	Q						
45+				T	S					
40+			U							
40−										

Retest score

The long cigar shape produced by the plots in Table A1 implies good reliability. High scores on the original test are predicting high scores on the retest. The lower scores are less good predictors but the trend is close to a diagonal line.

To calculate a figure for the reliability of the test we need to correlate the two sets of test scores. There are many ways to do this, and many pocket-size calculators are capable of carrying out the procedure. The simplest way to estimate the reliability is to rearrange the plots into four quadrants:

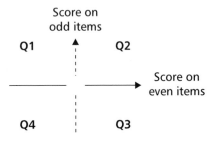

If the testing situation has high reliability, the plots should fall into the quadrants Q2 and Q4 ie high/high or low/low.

The dividing lines for the quadrants are provided by the means (the average scores for the tests). The mean mark of the original test is 59.9, and for the retest it is 58.9.

The quadrants are thus:

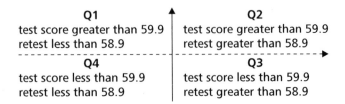

Plotting our scores into these four quadrants gives:

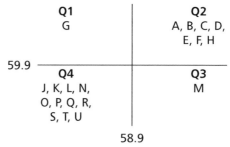

Now we are ready for our simple calculation. Multiply the number of plots in Q2 by those in Q4 and then divide this number by Q1 multiplied by Q3.

$$\frac{Q2 \times Q4}{Q1 \times Q3} = \frac{7 \times 11}{1 \times 1} = \frac{77}{1} = 77$$

This figure of 77 can be compared with those in a simple table to give an estimate of reliability.

Q2 × Q4/Q1 × Q3 =	4	6	8.5	15	21	34	71
Reliability =	0.5	0.6	0.7	0.8	0.85	0.9	0.95

Our testing situation has a reliability of slightly better than 0.95, which is satisfactory. Indeed it is difficult to produce tests of ability that have higher levels of reliability than this.

It should be clear from this example that it is not possible to produce an exact rank order of ability from test results that are samples. We have a reliable testing situation but the estimated rank order on the original test is not the same as that on the retest. It is also very difficult to draw a line and say, 'Candidates who score below this figure will fail.' Suppose we were to decide that 50 was the pass mark, who would 'fail'? On the sample of ability in the 'test', candidates S, T, and U. On the sample of ability estimated by the retest, candidates J, O, P, R, and U.

Split-half reliability

The test and retest method of establishing reliability is widely used to develop psychometric tests of ability. It is, however, impractical as a procedure for checking the reliability of tests used in training. It is not a sensible use of training time to go through the whole procedure of testing twice. A more practical (although rather less accurate) way of estimating the reliability of a test is to use the 'split-half' method. In this the scores on the odd numbered items (questions 1, 3, 5 etc) in the test are added together and plotted as above for 'test' scores. The scores on even numbered items (questions 2, 4, 6 etc) are added together and treated as the 'retest' scores.

Suppose we have an objective test on 'product knowledge' and we use it to estimate the knowledge of 10 of our sales staff. The test has 80 items and each correct item scores one mark. The maximum possible scores are 40 for odd items and 40 for even items. Our 10 staff score as follows:

Candidate	A	B	C	D	E	F	G	H	J	K
Total score	77	76	74	73	69	67	67	54	46	42
Odd items correct	38	39	36	38	33	35	33	24	26	20
Even items correct	39	37	38	35	36	32	34	30	20	22

Totals: Odd items   322
        Even items   323

Means: Odd items   32.2
        Even items   32.3

Plot the 10 candidates into the four quadrants

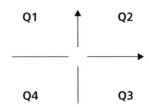

Now calculate the value of$= \dfrac{Q2 \times Q4}{Q1 \times Q3}$

Note: an empty quadrant takes the value of 1 and this avoids the division of a sum by 0 (which would result in infinity).

Is the test sufficiently reliable?

(The worked example is over the page, but it is better to try it for yourself before looking at that.)

Improving reliability

It will never be possible to achieve absolute reliability when testing ability by use of samples. Reliability can be improved by increasing the size of the sample. This means that if the estimated reliability falls below 0.8, more test items need to be written to increase the length of the test and thus the size of the sample of the ability being assessed.

It is also possible to improve reliability by standardising the test conditions – the physical conditions, the instructions and so on.

A third factor that affects reliability is the marking system. Improvements can usually be made to the scoring system by using trained observers, or subject specialists. The use of detailed marking guides is also recommended.

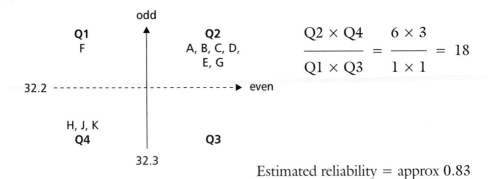

$$\frac{Q2 \times Q4}{Q1 \times Q3} = \frac{6 \times 3}{1 \times 1} = 18$$

Estimated reliability = approx 0.83

Index